COMBING
THE
COAST

COMBING THE COAST

San Francisco to Santa Cruz

A Lively Guide to Beaches,
Backroads, Parks,
Historic Sites and Towns

Ruth A. Jackson

Chronicle Books
San Francisco

Library of Congress Cataloging in Publication Data
Jackson, Ruth A.
    Combing the coast, San Francisco to Santa Cruz.

    Includes index.
    1. California—Description and travel—1951- —
Guide-books.   I. Title.
F859.3.J33   917.94'6   81-2272
ISBN 0-87701-140-0   AACR2

Edited by Suzanne Lipsett.
Book and cover design by Paula Schlosser.
Cartography by Milne.
Composition by HMS Typography.

Chronicle Books
870 Market Street
San Francisco, CA 94102

Photo credits

Front cover: Hal Lauritzen
Back cover: Ruth A. Jackson

Ed Brady: 17
Edna Bullock: 59,69,81
Jim Fee: 44,93
Ruth A. Jackson: 14, 15, 21, 26, 32, 37, 38, 42,
    46, 47, 55, 57, 60, 63, 64, 71, 74, 82 , 83,
    88, 90, 92, 94, 96, 97
National Park Service photos by Dick Frear:
    title page, 11, 13, 18, 26
Santa Cruz Chamber of Commerce: 105, 107,
    109, 110
Donna Starr: 29, 30
State Highway: Department 36

Ruth A. Jackson lives in a small home perched on Albany Hill in the East Bay. Besides her freelance writing, Monday through Thursday, she commutes to a job as an advertising copywriter in San Francisco. Friday mornings she is packed and ready to take off to a shack overlooking the Pacific near Half Moon Bay. From here she has spent many years investigating the legends and lore and exploring the highways and backroads of this coastal area that she knows and loves so well.

Contents

A Few Events to Watch for Along the Coast

January (Also December and February). Migration south of the great gray whales. See pages 25, 35, and 103 for best lookout spots.

February Driftwood and pebble hunting excellent if storms have cooperated.

March Wild flowers have their big scene all along the coast.

May Mussel quarantine begins on May 1.
Portuguese Chamarita parade and free barbecue in Pescadero, usually six weeks after Easter.
Portuguese Chamarita parade and free barbecue in Half Moon Bay, usually seven weeks after Easter.

June The beaches are still relatively uncrowded. Get out!

July Bass Derby (through August) in Pacifica to celebrate the striped bass runs.
Coastside Country Fair & Rodeo, Half Moon Bay, July 4th weekend.
La Honda Days Celebration and Barbeque, July 4th.

August Pacifica Frontier Days, last week in August.

September Artichoke Festival, Pescadero: food, art, antiques; Labor Day.
Kings Mountain Art & Craft Fair, 6 miles south of Highway 92 and #35 junction, Labor Day weekend.

October Reservations start for elephant seal tours to Año Nuevo, telephone 415/348-SEAL for Sam Trans tours. See page 98.
Welcome Back Monarch (butterfly) Day, Natural Bridges State Park, 2nd or 3rd week in October.
Pumpkin season in full glory, well worth a roll of color film. Prices aren't that much lower, but you've a bigger choice.
Mussel Quarantine usually ends October 31. Check 415/843-7900 to be sure.

November December Dramatic storms perhaps, but clear, tranquil days in between.

Preface

COMBING THE COAST is for those who like to explore for a day or a weekend. And the comparatively unknown coastline from San Francisco to Santa Cruz, with its coastal mountains, small towns, and big redwood parks, is ideal for quiet, leisurely enjoyment.

Whatever your special interests, you'll probably find them listed here. Beachcombing, antiques and crafts, fishing, horseback riding, dining, wildlife and bird watching, sunbathing and swimming at nude beaches, golfing, hiking, and biking: this is just a start on the activities waiting for you. Use the index of this book as your gold mine and dig out the pastimes that appeal to you.

But times change. Although listings were checked right up to press time, you may discover that the "find" of a restaurant or art gallery has changed hands or that the Victorian house you were counting on has been demolished. I hope such incidents will be rare and suffered with understanding.

One of the many delightful facets of the countryside covered here—so close to the San Francisco Bay Area and the Peninsula—is that you can enjoy it all year. From early September until the rainy season (usually November through February) and from the end of the rains until Memorial Day, the weather is at its glorious best. But each month has its magic days when the call of the ocean, mountains and open road is irresistible.

When those days come, here's to happy adventures combing the California coast from San Francisco to the edge of Santa Cruz.

Ruth A. Jackson

From San Francisco to Pacifica

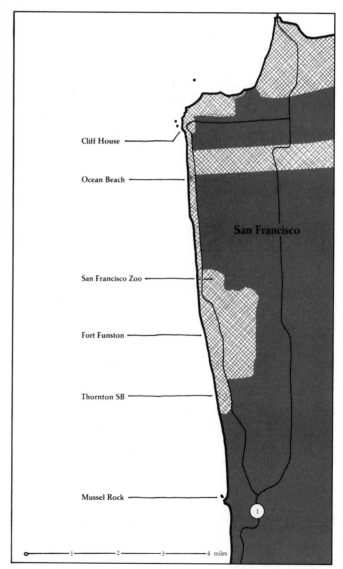

1

Cliff House

Ocean Beach

San Francisco

San Francisco Zoo

Fort Funston

Thornton SB

Mussel Rock

1

1 — 2 — 3 — 4 miles

I T'S ALL THERE within close and easy on the budget range, ready to be enjoyed for an hour, a day, or a weekend. There's the sea itself, that great expanse of Pacific Ocean at the edge of the continent. Inland are the green-gold foothills, the backroads, and the big redwood parks. The seasoning consists of the small, individualistic towns along the way.

the weather

One of the many bonuses of combing the beautiful stretch of coastline between San Francisco and Pacifica is that you can enjoy it all year. Even the fog that mutes harsh edges can be soothing. The best months for this area are usually in early spring and late fall, when the days are clear and the temperature is crisp to surprisingly warm. After Memorial Day until around Labor Day you can expect some fog, but it usually clears in the afternoon, and if you plan your route carefully you might avoid it entirely. Along Skyline Boulevard, that winding Highway 35 on the spine of the coastal hills, you'll get more fog. One resident who kept track discovered that in addition to rain, five inches of moisture dripped off trees here each year. South of Daly City, inland areas—including the big redwood parks—are often sunny even when a cotton batting of fog clings to the shoreline and skyline. Beaches vary in this regard. In Pacifica you may be discouraged by impenetrable fog just south of Mussel Rock and then find Pedro Point, a few miles farther south, bathed in sunshine. Near Santa Cruz the sun has usually arrived before you do.

As for winter rains—late November through February—they wash the air to give you those glorious clear days in-between. Besides, unless you melt in rain, why not don rubber boots, rain gear, and enjoy? This is the time the prized driftwood, fishing floats, and other booty wash in, and you may have miles of beach all to yourself.

the drama of storms and sunsets

Please don't wait only for calm days, or you will miss the drama of a storm at sea. As you stand, bundled up against the rain and biting wind, or sit protected in your car, you will feel the immense presence of the ocean, as wave after wave thunders in, perhaps even hurling surf across Highway 1. Afterwards, walking on the wet, shining sand among driftwood and shredded seaweed can be as peaceful as a benediction.

Of course, all along this coastline you have the magic chance to see and compare sunsets. Perhaps on a crystal-clear dusk you may glimpse the rare but vivid emerald, or "liquid jade," color for one split second before the sunset colors disappear. Even after dark, the ocean can be mesmerizing, especially when the waves are edged with microorganisms that make them flourescent. Microorganisms, incidentally, may also be responsible for the foam that sometimes billows along the surf line—unfortunately, though, this same phenomenon can be caused by pollution from detergents.

All right, you're set to start your ad-

venture along the coast south from San Francisco.

But whether you're biking, driving, or taking public transportation, why not treat yourself to the four-plus miles of San Francisco's exhilarating—that is, breezy— *Ocean Beach*, presided over by *Cliff House*, just south of the spot where ships head in towards the Golden Gate?

Ocean Beach

To reach the Cliff House area from downtown San Francisco, drive straight west on Geary Boulevard and park in the sizeable parking area to the north. If you're

directions

San Francisco's Ocean Beach stretches along the wave-lapped strand for four wind-swept miles.

busing, take the 38 Geary to the end or call 673-MUNI for alternate transportation.

This is great country for biking, too. Part of the *Pacific Coast Bikecentennial Route*, popular with cyclists, runs from San Francisco to Santa Cruz. For maps and information, send $1.00 to the Division of Highways, 1120 N. Street, Sacramento, CA 95814, or call 916/323-2544.

cycling

Cliff House

Since 1863, millions of tourists have visited the series of Cliff Houses that have been built here and burned down. The first burned in 1887 when a schooner loaded with dynamite foundered on the rocks below. On the outside, the present Cliff House is squat and forgettable, although its present owner, the Golden Gate Recreation Area, plans to bring it back to its 1906 glory (unfortunately, not the many-storied Gingerbread Palace, which was the 1905 version). Cliff House is worth visiting even before the makeup job is finished,

San Francisco's Cliff House is a good spot to start your tour down the coast.

though, for the view from its oceanside windows and concrete terraces is unforgettable. On a clear day you can see west eighteen miles to the Farallon Islands, north along the entire Marin coast to Point Reyes, and south to Pacifica's Pedro Point. If you want a higher vantage point and quieter atmosphere, walk up past two huge stone lions to Sutro Heights, to the east of Cliff House.

California sea lions congregate on Seal Rocks, within view of San Francisco's Cliff House.

seals and sea lions Another irresistible attraction, for you and for the tourists who pile in and out of the chartered buses that snort up to the curb here, are the gulls, pelicans and other sea birds that rest on nearby Seal Rocks— and, of course, the rocks' larger tenants. Unless it is late June or July, when the pinnipeds (mammals with flippers that eat flesh) have gone to offshore islands to mate, you'll hear their wet, deep barking and see a lot of close-up action. These black mammals, which you'll see draped on the rocks, are the same "seals" that cavort around in circuses and zoos. Actually, these particular pinnipeds are California sea lions—more agile than seals because they can rotate their hind flippers. The flippers of a true seal are fixed behind like a tail so the animal has to undulate and flop forward like a worm. Another tip, if you see external ears, it's a sea lion, not a seal.

Boisterous Steller's sea lions, usually tawny in color and bigger than California sea lions (bulls can weigh a ton), also have those outside ears. The smallest and shyest pinnipeds, spotted harbor or leopard seals, prefer protected waters, although a few may haul themselves out here and on small rocks further south. If you do spot any, chances are their big brown eyes will be regarding you with as much curiosity as you show gazing at them. Probably the most exciting pinnipeds along this coast are the mammoth elephant seals, "the world's most improbable animals." Bulls can weigh over three tons, and the male's elephantlike proboscis, or snout, helps him give out a bellow you can hear for miles. You'll meet them close up at Año Nuevo Point, farther south, almost at the Santa Cruz County line.

whales The biggest sea mammals you'll see— if you're lucky—are the gray whales, during their migrations in December into February and March through April. The sight of pods of whales spouting, flapping their tails, and occasionally gyrating out of the water is unforgettable. You might see a

The shy harbor seal is sometimes seen along beaches, but more frequently in harbors and sloughs.

few from Cliff House. Farther south are many exposed headlands where you can stand and watch them with binoculars. Look for their spouts, or spumes, as they surface to blow before sounding. At Pacifica's municipal pier you might see them only a hundred yards away.

distressed marine mammals As you're combing this coast, if you see a distressed marine mammal, the California Marine Mammal Center, Fort Cronkite, California 94965, suggests these rules.

1. Do not touch the animal. Some mothers abandon babies because of the human scent.

2. Call the C.M.M.C. rescue line (415/561-7284) immediately.
3. Observe the animal from a distance and keep others away while you're waiting for the rescue crew.
4. If possible, stay to assist the crew.

Other wildlife rehabilitation groups to call if you see distressed animals or birds are:

Peninsula Humane Society
12 Airport Boulevard
San Mateo, CA 94401
415/573-3785

Wildlife Rescue, Inc.
4037 El Camino Way
Palo Alto, CA 94306
415/494-SAVE

Native Wildlife Rescue
2200 7th Avenue
Santa Cruz, CA 95062
408/462-0726

There are many things to do and see near the Cliff House before you head south along the coast. You'll want to glance at the ruins of the old Sutro Baths, where as many as twenty-four thousand people at one time could enjoy bathing in its many elaborate hot to cold pools. The mostly deserted facility burned in the 1960s, but some of its antique musical and other coin-operated machines are now on view in a Cliff House museum. If plans materialize, the Sutro ruins will blossom into gardens. **Sutro Baths**

Another relic—this from the days when the Amusement Park flourished across the highway with its Loop-the-Loop and Laughing Sal—is the thirty-year-old

camera obscura Giant Camera, mounted on a concrete terrace below Cliff House. This rare attraction, housed in a garish building shaped like a box camera, is a camera obscura, built after a design by Leonardo da Vinci. Its revolving eye takes pictures of the whole sweep of view and reflects it all inside on a huge dishlike object. This view—in some ways more encompassing than the one outside—is certainly worth the small admission fee.

For the next dozen miles south of Cliff House, the ocean beach is definitely no-frills. Take advantage of the last touches of civilization—like restrooms, telephones, bars, a souvenir shop that sells film, plus restaurants—before you leave. You'll find some of these conveniences close by to the south, but not all together.

All year long, wide, sandy Ocean Beach is usually crowded with picnickers, strollers and their frisking dogs, for this is one of San Francisco's favorite escapes. You'll see few people in swimming, however. The surf is treacherous and the water too cold.

the sea— a warning *A warning before you venture along this or any coast:* that tranquil, rhythmic surf can be misleading. Those wise to the ways of the sea try to keep an eye always on incoming waves even if they are just strolling on the beach. It's not true, as rumor has it, that every seventh wave is dangerous, but there are occasional killer waves. You could be standing with your back to the ocean when a killer wave or a Big Roller twice as mountainous as other waves rises up out of a heavy sea. As it smashes against the sand or rocks it could

Camera Obscura offers sweeping views of ocean panorama and nearby Seal Rocks.

scoop you away into roiling water where another wave might sweep over you again or pound you to mincemeat against rocks.

If you're brave or foolhardy enough to go swimming, rip tides, especially on incoming tides, are another hazard. Rip tides are a legacy of the winter storms that batter against and chew up sandy shores. Until July or August, when the waves again build up the gentle, sandy slopes, much of the sand is deposited in sandbars off shore. Waves that break over these bars are trapped; when they find an opening they surge through in a powerful funnel. If you're in the vicinity of this surge, you could be swept out to sea in chill water, ranging in temperature from the high forties to low fifties. If you do become caught in a rip tide, don't fight the current, experts advise; swim at right angles to the

rip tides

tide and parallel to shore until the rip tide feathers out and you can make it in.

sea cave hazards

As important is the warning to stay out of sea caves, where you could really become trapped if the ocean turns treacherous. Too many people living along the "Pacific" have encountered dead bodies washed up on shore. They know that even at low tide the ocean may turn on the careless.

shoreline erosion

All along the coast, the shoreline is eroding away, receding anywhere from an inch to several inches a year. If the improved San Francisco sewer to the ocean is finally built, all sand excavated in the project may be dumped west of the Great Highway in the hopes of keeping Ocean Beach more secure.

Four miles south of Cliff House, at the northern boundary of Fort Funston, is a parking lot on the ocean side of the highway. From here it's an easy incline to the beach, and the cliff to the south is pockmarked with sandy caves and indentations where you can bask, out of the wind, when the sun is shining.

Golden Gate Park

As you drive that four miles, you'll pass the tip of San Francisco's Golden Gate Park, with its miles of greenery, small lakes and recreation facilities, but that's another story. The Dutch windmill at the edge of the park to the north is now being rehabilitated through private donations.

San Francisco Zoo

Another popular spot with all ages, three to 103, is the San Francisco Zoo, just off Sloat Boulevard to your left. Besides the usual lions, tigers, elephants, and such, there's a children's zoo with domesticated animals visiting children can pet. A small train with guide meanders throughout the zoo grounds, a boon for the footsore.

Fort Funston

If it's been a while since you've driven along the Great Highway south of the point at which it turns into Skyline Boulevard, you'll be surprised at the changes the Golden Gate National Recreational Area administration has wrought at *Fort Funston.* A well-marked paved road leads you into a big parking area. From here you can stroll to the edge of the high cliffs to watch kites being maneuvered or graceful and colorful hang gliders take off and land. That is, you'll see all this if the wind is ten miles an hour or more. (There's a demonstration wind machine geared to produce some electricity where you can check the velocity.) If it's one of those rare windless, nonfoggy days, enjoy. Picnic, find a niche in the sand above the cliffside where you can sunbathe, or clamber down the steep path to the ocean. Among other Fort Funston niceties are phones, restrooms, benches, a senior citizens' clubhouse, and a truck that vends snacks and hotdogs on weekends. There's also a wheelchair-accessible loop trail that covers a gentle 1.5 miles of coastal scenery. Look the other way from the sea and you'll see the backside of the San Francisco skyline.

little boxes

Whether you stay on Highway 1 through San Francisco, start south along the sweep of Ocean Beach, or go west on Highway 35, you'll get tantalizing glimpses of the ocean, but rows of "ticky-tacky" houses creeping over those foothills will also assault your eyes. These are the houses that inspired Malvina Reynold's hit tune "Little Boxes." The subsequent pub-

licity upset the Daly City fathers, but it was too late to stem the pastel tide.

stables   For a change of pace, why not climb on a horse to investigate the trails that overlook the ocean here? You can rent horses just north of the junction of Alemany Boulevard with Highway 35, at the Palo Mar Stables or the St. Francis Riding Academy next door.

Aerial view above Daly City shows residential subdivisions spreading down the valley toward the coast.

If you can't wait to take off your shoes and stroll on ocean-washed sand, take the well-marked turnoff here to *Thornton Beach State Park*. From San Francisco you can also drive directly here along Westlake Boulevard off Highway 280. After de-   **Thornton Beach State Park**

A lonely stretch of surf-crashed sand reaches from Thornton Beach to Mussel Rock near Pacifica.

scending a hairpin half-mile, pay $2.00 a car, and park. Why pay when you can park for nothing at some beaches further south? There are restrooms! And if you're early enough on a weekend, your car will sit on nondusty asphalt. Also, the rangers on duty will answer your questions and help out in emergencies. There are other extras, such as self-guided nature trails and rangers who can often be talked into identifying native shrubs and wildflowers, and describing the owls and other wildlife that flourish here, so close to the crowded city.

This beautiful beach is kept scrupulously clean; you've probably discovered that clean beaches are rare. "Why," asked a ranger, "can picnickers carry full cans of beer to the beach and not have the strength to tote away empty cans?"

The thirty-five picnic tables (with stoves and water) at Thornton Beach have the distinction of being right on top of that line where the San Andreas Fault meets the

San Andreas Fault

sea. As you drive down into the park, to your left you'll see where huge hunks of old Highway 1 crumbled off in the 1957 landslide as well as many other indications of slides and other kinds of damage from the 1906 and 1957 earthquakes. What will happen and where will you land if the next quake strikes while you're eating hotdogs at a picnic table here? Chances are remote, but. . . .

Mussel Rock

The beach stretches north to San Francisco's Ocean Beach, a healthy hike if you have the stamina. Going south toward *Mussel Rock,* you may find fossils of whalebone, seashells, and rare sand dollars in the sides of the bluffs. Some of these fossils, over a million years old, have been uncovered by earthquakes and slides.

The farther south you go, the more fishermen (or eternal optimists) you are likely to meet than beachcombers, so chances are good that you may find an interesting piece of driftwood, a cork float, or glass ground into white and green gemlike pieces.

Mussel Rock is a breezy two-mile hike from Thornton State Beach headquarters. Provided the cliffsides are dry, if you are adventurous and part mountain goat, you can take a trail that drops to the ocean about midway between the two points. This goat trail starts at Daly City's tiny *Northridge Park* (on Northridge Drive, which loops around from Skyline Drive). Coming south, take Westmoor Avenue to Skyline Drive, which parallels Highway 35. From Pacifica (the next town south), take the Paloma turnoff and continue north until you intersect with Skyline

Drive. Or call SamTrans (San Mateo County Transit) Information (415/871-2200) to find out how you can get there by bus.

Buddhist Center Academy

Walk under an arch on the ocean side of the parking lot by the Nichiren Shoshu Buddhist Center Academy, a community center where people meet for "study, discussions, chanting and other activities to help each other." The center is usually open from 9 A.M. to 10 P.M., and visitors are welcome (415/992-1316). Notice how tiny the figures on the beach below appear. Stand for a while to watch gulls who have caught the updraft soar noiselessly by without moving their wings. Or perhaps you'll see graceful hang gliders with their human cargo or streamers of pelicans. Notice, too, that though the sun may be shining on the sea below the updraft is bringing up moist sea air and turning it into chill fog (yes, too often).

If you're still insistent on living dangerously and trying the trail, start out to the right of the arch and hope you won't slide on the wide, steep portion halfway down, where the gravel acts like ball bearings.

Daly City Dump

A much easier way to get to Mussel Rock is to park in the big lot near the Daly City transfer station—in plain terms, the dump. From the north, continue on Skyline Drive, which curves down, until you see the entrance sign. Coming from Pacifica, take the Paloma turnoff and continue north. Don't let the name dump or its purpose bother you. This is not an old smelly dump with gulls hovering over it; the building is discreetly tucked away, almost out of sight, and the view from the large parking lot is one of the most spectacular along the San Mateo coast. You can see west to the arc of the horizon, south to Pedro Point and, if the day is crystal clear, north to Point Reyes. Walk through an opening in the sturdy wire fence past a sign welcoming pedestrians but prohibiting motorized vehicles. From then on the wide path zigs and zags easily down to the beach and rocks.

The beach is a lovely sandy stretch, a good place for gazing at and listening to the roaring sea. It is also fine for strolling unless you arrive at the same time (usually late in May) as hundreds of thousands of *Vellela lata*—commonly called jellyfish. These purplish-blue hydroids grow to four inches long and have a graceful, diagonal saillike fin on top. They resemble the Portuguese man-of-war. Luckily they're not identical, and therefore are not poisonous. However, vellela are sticky underfoot, and they smell. Eventually they dry up, and all is forgotten until winds blow them ashore to litter the beach again the following year.

Velella lata (jellyfish)

Fishing is an important coastside activity and Thornton Beach has the first sizeable stretch of ocean-fishing coast south of San Francisco.

ocean fishing

Before you load up your gear, be sure you have three items to make your fishing legal and more profitable. First, you need a California fishing license, available at most big sporting goods stores ($5.00 a year for ocean fishing only, with additional charges for salmon and trout stickers).

Next, pick up a tide table early in the year, also available at sporting goods stores and bait shops, or at many coastside service stations. Tide tables are calculated for a definite location—usually San Francisco's Golden Gate. The farther south you go, the more time you must subtract, following the correction provided on the table. Near Half Moon Bay, for example, tides ebb and flow about an hour earlier than the tables show; if the tide table reports a low tide at 8 A.M., low tide at Half Moon Bay beaches will actually occur around 7 A.M.

Order the next item by mail: Ocean Fishing Map number 53, for San Francisco, San Mateo, and Santa Cruz counties, from the Office of Procurement, Publications Section, P.O. Box 1015, North Highlands, CA 95660. For $1.00 you will get an easy-to-follow map as well as advice on where, how, and with what to fish. Even experienced anglers might pick up pointers. (The map for Monterey south is number 54.)

Statistics show that the most fish per hour are caught from skiffs or party boats, but pier fishing and especially surf fishing are more popular.

The calmest and warmest periods along the shore occur during early spring and late fall before the northwesterly winds start blowing. However, from May through October, even in fog or wind, fishermen catch the most striped bass when they cast into and beyond the breakers. Stripers usually weigh from five to eight pounds, although some caught here have weighed in at fifty pounds.

Other fish you can catch from the shore are surf perch, jacksmelt, white croaker, flounder, sand sole, shark, and ray. For surf perch, cast out into the breakers, let the bait sink almost to the bottom, and reel in slack. You'll have no problem knowing when you get a bite. Surf perch are fighters, and you may have to work to drag them and your sinker through heavy surf. Keep your line taut when you're reeling one in. Surf perch travel in schools and are voracious eaters; if you manage—by hit-and-miss casting—to catch one, you'll probably get others in the vicinity. Some authorities insist that an incoming tide is best; others say it makes little difference.

You need heavy gear for striped bass (at least a 12-pound test line and a pole from 10.5 to 11 feet long), but you can catch jacksmelt and surf perch with small hooks, even on hand lines. Throwing bread into the water may make these schooling fish congregate.

surf-fishing tips Another tip for catching the big ones: look for flocks of birds diving for and feeding on anchovies. You can be quite sure that striped bass or salmon are feeding below and forcing those anchovies up to the surface. This is why many fishermen swear by live anchovies as bait. But many also rig their lines so they can quickly change to lure fishing at the first indication that stripers are about. For these fish they use metal spoons, leadhead, or squid, and cast out a good distance.

rock-fishing tips This southern part of Thornton Beach will give you your first taste of rock fishing, although you may find many areas further south more profitable. Besides steady legs and sturdy equipment, you

A beachcomber's assortment of treasures includes two pincushion-like shells of sea urchins.

need patience. Casting must be timed to surf action; hooks and sinkers are likely to get tangled up in rocks, kelp, or seaweed, so have a good supply of hooks. If the bottom is rough you might use cheap sinkers—even old bolts, spark plugs, or sand-filled tobacco sacks will do. The catch here will be cabezon, ling cod, and other rockfish, all of which can be whoppers.

If you're set for clamming, you won't dig the coastside although further south you'll be able to scratch for littleneck clams in the gravel at Año Nuevo Point.

mussels Vitamin-rich mussels are common all along the coastside. They're a tasty but neglected shellfish, treasured by many Europeans, including Portola and his explorers, who passed this way in 1769.

Since Mussel Rock is at the south end

of Thornton Beach, this is a handy place to mention the how-tos of mussel getting and cooking.

First a reminder: you need a valid California fishing license for clam digging or mussel prying.

Then a warning: mussels (and clams to a lesser extent) can contain poison during summer months, when they get a deadly toxin from the organism called Gonyaulax, which gives the ocean a reddish color when it's about in great numbers. The mussels filter it in for food. Mussels are quarantined from May through October, sometimes longer. Check with the Sanitary Engineers, California Public Health Department in Berkeley (415/843-7900) for safe periods. Don't take chances; the toxin can cause lethal nerve paralysis. Since California abalone, crab, and shrimp don't feed on the poison-producing Gonyaulax, there's no danger from eating them during the summer and fall months. And if you get your mussels in a pollution-free area during the legal season, don't worry. Just savor.

Plan to do your mussel gathering when the tide is really low so the maximum number of rocks will be exposed. Mussels attach themselves with strong whiskers to rocks at the midtide zone. Pry them loose with a tire iron or similar tool, knock off the barnacles, scrape off other encrusted sea creatures with a knife or stiff brush, and wash them several times to get rid of **how to cook** sand. Then drain the mussels for at least **mussels** half an hour, and steam them in a pot with garlic, green onions, parsley, butter, and a dash of white wine. Dish them out the min-ute they open or they may turn as tough as tire rubber.

Those ornate Cliff House rooms over- **motels** looking the crashing surf and wheeling gulls are no more. A small motel, *Seal Rock Inn* (415/752-8000) a few blocks east of Cliff House, at Point Lobos and 48th, does have a sea view. A fraction of that view is also visible from their restaurant, which serves breakfast and lunch, with an emphasis on omelets.

Two motels in the Ocean Beach/zoo area are the *Ocean Park Motel* (415/566-7020) and *Roberts at the Beach Motel* (415/564-2610).

For additional information on motels, hotels, and RV parks, contact the San Francisco Convention and Visitors Bureau, 1390 Market Street, San Francisco, CA 94102. Or pick up a San Francisco Lodging Guide and other tourist information from the bureau's center at Hallidie Plaza, Powell and Market streets, on the lower plaza.

If you're on a strict budget and adven- turous, the *San Francisco International* **youth hostel** *Hostel* (415/771-4646), part of the American Youth Hostel, Inc., has accommodations for ninety-six in a historic Civil War barracks at Fort Mason. Enter the fort at Franklin and Bay. The view is inspiring, one of the best in the city, and the hostel organization encourages you not to be put off by the word youth—all ages are welcome. Still, since the accommodations are in dormitories for four or eight and there is an 11 P.M. curfew plus other restrictions, few oldsters pay the modest fee to be put up.

where to eat   At Cliff House, the *Sea Food and Beverage Company* (415/386-3330), open at 11 A.M., specializes in sunset watching, fresh netted seafood, and Sunday brunch. Upstairs at the Cliff House (415/387-5847) you'll find more modest prices. The upstairs establishment opens for breakfast at 9 A.M. every day of the year, providing a pleasant start to your adventure south. The menu includes forty varieties of omelets. For lunch, the half-pound hamburger with salad, fruit, and frills should fill even a teenage boy. This restaurant also serves dinner.

A series of smaller restaurants is strung up the curve above Cliff House, so there's no danger of starvation. However, if you can, do squeeze in to Cliff House; you'll have no regrets.

2

From Pacifica
to Devil's Slide

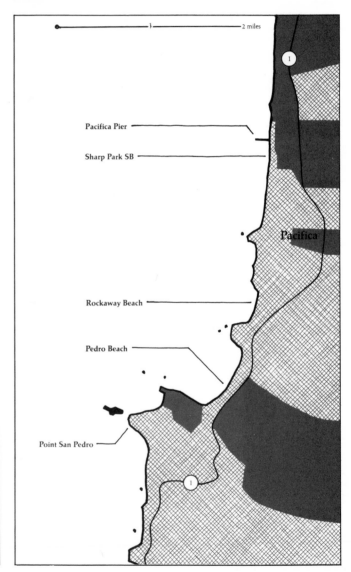

A BUMPER STICKER much favored by its somewhat defensive inhabitants reads, "Where the hell is Pacifica?"

Actually, Pacifica starts 2.2 miles south of the Thornton Beach turnoff. The present town, a sprawling 12.6 square miles, gobbled up several smaller communities in 1957 and suffered many growing pains to achieve its present population of 39,000.

Worth a glimpse to your left across the highway, just before the Paloma Avenue turnoff, is Anderson's nostalgic red-colored, two-story general store, built in 1901.

The forbidding looking castle on the hill, also to your left, was modeled after a Scottish royal dwelling, and built of concrete and steel to withstand earthquakes. Completed in 1908, its varied past includes stints as an abortion mill in the 1920s, as a speakeasy during Prohibition, and later as a Coast Guard headquarters. It is now a private residence, owned by Sam Mazza, who has filled the rooms with funky collectibles. Mazza will occasionally let organized charitable groups use the castle to sample its unusual ambience and enjoy the view. He can be contacted through the Pacifica Chamber of Commerce, (415/355-4122).

Pacifica Pier   Next? Even if you're not intending to catch a big salmon or several crabs for dinner, the L-shaped *Pacifica Municipal Pier,* which juts 1020 feet over crashing surf, is worth a visit for panoramic views of the coast and close-up glimpses of sea birds and whales.

To reach the pier from Highway 1, take the Paloma turnoff; turn left on Palmetto Avenue, right on San Jose, and find a place to park. If you've passed the Sea Urchin Saloon (country music Friday and Saturday nights) or the Amused Carrot Co-op, you've gone too far. Or take the Paloma turnoff and continue to Beach Boulevard before turning left. Don't fret; 1020 feet of pier is hard to miss.

Ignore the signs about closing hours; there are none, and some excellent catches have been made at night. Out on the pier are fish-cleaning sinks and benches. Other amenities include well-ventilated restrooms plus a bait shop that sells cold sandwiches, snacks, and beer.

The clientele here is varied; you'll hear many languages and dialects as you walk to the end. Clothing is informal, with windbreakers de rigueur.

Views? On a clear day (unfortunately, usually windy) you can see to the blue horizon, framed on your right by San Francisco's Golden Gate and, even farther north, Point Reyes. To the south is nearby Gray Whale Point, named for the giant mammals (up to forty tons) that migrate south from the Bering Sea to Baja California, from the last of November into February, returning with their calves in March or April. During these weeks and occasionally earlier or later a few of these mammoth creatures swim right under the pier. One of the rangers believes they

the whale spectacle

Pacifica Pier jutting out beyond the crashing surf, is a popular platform for fishing and whale watching.

are attracted by food—perhaps grass shrimp—about two hundred yards to the south. Some of the whales even rub their bellies on the sand nearby to rid themselves of the barnacles that give them the gray look. (Actually, they start out life black.) Unless you take an excursion to Lower California during the whale's winter mating season, this is probably as close as you'll get to these exciting fellow mammals.

Many sea birds, including gulls, cormorants, and pelicans, keep a sharp eye on the activity here. As always, it is a thrill to see the ungainly looking brown pelicans plunge, like graceful dive bombers, into the surf to stun their prey. They are often closely followed by gulls or terns who try to snatch the catch before the pelicans can manipulate the fish into their beaks. And you can see this whole show from the pier.

Fishing, of course, is the main reason

why as many as six hundred people at one time line up along the Pacifica Pier. Catches here have varied from small kingfish, flounder, and perch to a 37-pound salmon, a 43-pound bass, and a 60-pound halibut. And you don't even need a license to try on a public pier.

Most fishermen are early risers for good reason. Early mornings on an incoming tide (remember that tide table) should bring you luck, and if you hit this combination on a windless day, the odds are even better.

pier fishing tips Without a net, hoisting record-size catches like these the considerable distance from the waterline onto the pier can be heartbreaking if the hook rips out of the fish's mouth. So why not bring along a crab net to use for those crucial moments when you're landing your prize? Besides, you might snare some crabs if the big fish aren't biting. All the other equipment you really need is a saltwater rod and reel, leader, sinkers, a tide table, bucket or container for your catch, and your favorite fish knife. For bait most fishermen on the pier use pile worms that they buy at the pier bait shop, but a few prefer anchovies and mussels. Although a number 2 hook seems to work well for most fish here, those after the big salmon or stripers during their summer runs may use a big 3/0 hook or just a metal lure. Some experts swear by hooks as small as a number 6. Their theory: you're sure to catch small fish and there's always the chance a big one will grab one of those small fish. A few optimists catch small ones at the shallow end of the pier, and then move to the deep end with the live wiggling bait they've just caught.

This last maneuver illustrates a paradox of pier fishing. A luckless fisherman can be standing without a bite within a few feet of another one bringing in two or three fish at a time. The small crescent-shaped area at the end of the pier before it turns into its "L" often seems a lucky spot for buckets full of kingfish.

Incidentally, the large Spanish-type building with arched windows across Beach Boulevard to the south is not a convent or a discreet hotel. It is Pacifica's Sewage Treatment Plant, and the Pacifica City Council holds its meetings upstairs here.

The *Sharp Park Beach* turnoff is next, 3.2 miles south of the Pacifica boundary. If you like to hit a little white ball with a stick, take Clarendon Drive towards the ocean to the 18-hole *Sharp Park Golf Course*, often referred to as the "poor man's Pebble Beach." One kind phrase that has been used to describe this golf course is that it has potential. The putting greens are free, but you had better reserve by Monday to play the course on weekends; call 415/751-2997. If the coffee shop is closed, the snack bar carries survival rations.

Sharp Park Golf course

Ecologists and bird lovers enjoy the migratory waterfowl who use the few acres of swampy land in the golf course for nesting and wintering, but the birds may get in your way if you're a golfer. The same goes for the endangered San Francisco garter snake frequently found on the course. The snake is red with some blue and white on its back and a turquoise underside. It's live bearing—doesn't lay eggs but has baby snakes. Besides being endangered and beautiful, the snake is harmless.

For an easy-to-reach beach, drive or walk on past the golf course. The ocean's edge here is often lined with surf fishermen during the striped-bass season. Several years ago people driving in this area were surprised to see a large ship nuzzled against the golf course. This mishap almost cost the owners their cargo, for two men boarded the ship to claim salvage rights. After much newspaper furor and threats of legal action the men gave up their attempts.

Ocean Shore Railroad

Back to Highway 1, continue south for a mile. On your left, by a car wash, are the remains of a depot, the first visible remnant of the ill-fated *Ocean Shore Railroad*. Following the collapse of the railroad, this depot spent many distinguished years as the High Iron Restaurant. Eventually, the establishment was gutted by fire, and rebuilt as the present Vallemar Station. It's easily visible from the Reina del Mar turnoff. At present the restaurant is open only for Sunday brunch but the bar is open seven days a week. For more entertainment you can catch blues on Wednesday, jazz on Thursday, and rock music on Friday and Saturday.

The Ocean Shore Railroad was started in 1905. Ambitious plans called for a double-track line from San Francisco to Santa Cruz, clinging to the edges of coastside cliffs most of the way.

The 1906 quake destroyed most of the track and equipment. The railroad never recovered from this and numerous other misfortunes—landslides, rebuilding costs, and strikes, to name a few. Eventually, with passengers often seated on top of flat cars, a few trains rattled off from San Francisco on the "cool scenic route." At Tunitas Creek, where only a few crumbling concrete blocks from the trestle remain, passengers were transferred to a Stanley Steamer; they got back on a train at Swanton to chug into Santa Cruz. The trip was advertised as taking 5.5 hours, but it's doubtful if this schedule was ever kept. Although there is still an Ocean Shore Railroad office in San Francisco, the last trains under its banner ran in 1920.

Several other Ocean Shore Railroad depots remain; those at Pedro Point, Montara, and Half Moon Bay are now private homes; the one at El Granada is a real estate office.

With the collapse of the railroad, coastside hopes of hauling produce and of building up the tourist industry also collapsed.

Rockaway Beach

Rockaway Beach, just south of the depot, is a pleasant crescent of sand, often lined with fishermen during the run of stripers, some time after July 4th. The beach is flanked by a small motel and several restaurants: Italian, Chinese, Mexican, and American steak and seafood. Most of these eateries discourage bare feet. On Highway 1 immediately before the Rockaway Beach turnoff, there's a deli and a Colonel Sanders fast-food outlet.

On the landward side of Highway 1 at Crespi Drive, about three-fourths of a mile

Surf fishing rewards can be big when the striped bass are running off Rockaway Beach near Pacifica.

south of Rockaway Beach, is a state historical marker honoring Portola. Here's what it says, so you won't have to stop:

> Captain Gaspar de Portola camped October 31, 1769 by the Creek at the South of this valley. To that camp scouting parties brought news of a body of water to the East. On Nov. 4 the expedition advanced, turning inland. Here they climbed to the summit of Sweeney's Ridge and beheld, for the first time, the Bay of San Francisco.

At this writing, 1100 acres of *Sweeney Ridge* (note: Sweeney is without the 's)

were being taken over by the Golden Gate National Recreation Area, so access to this route of discovery will probably be easier in the future. For information check with Pacifica Parks and Recreation (415/877-8631).

The trail to the original discovery site starts at the end of Fassler Avenue, back in the Rockaway Beach area. Yes, the trail is steep in some places; the views on a clear day, plus the thrill of standing on the discovery spot are well worth the effort. Near the stone marker honoring Portola (close to a big green water tank) you can see in all directions—to the towers of the Golden Gate Bridge, Marin County, and the entire East Bay, with Mount Diablo and the hills as a backdrop. You'll also see, of course, the southern portion of the great San Francisco Bay, which Portola's group found. But one question has never been answered. Who was Sweeney? Did he run cattle on the hill? Was he one of the Irish who had come to this area to farm potatoes and cabbage? No one knows for sure.

On the ocean side, just past Crespi Drive, is the city-run *Pedro Beach*, a pleasant mix of sand and surf with *free* restrooms. There's also plenty of parking space, and the Pacifica police often allow overnight parking for self-contained RVs. Call them at 415/877-8612. Pedro Beach is a quick drive from San Francisco and easy to reach by public transportation also. SamTrans (415/573-2200) runs frequent buses that connect with BART (Bay Area Rapid Transit) in Daly City. Incidentally, those black shiny mammals bobbing in the

Sweeney Ridge— San Francisco Bay Discovery Site

Pedro Beach

Sweeney Ridge (where Portola first viewed the Bay) offers panoramic views along the coast and inland.

Sanchez Adobe in Pacifica has been restored and is open to the public Wednesdays and Sundays.

water are probably not seals, but human surfers.

the Sanchez Adobe

The *Sanchez Adobe* is less than a mile inland along the Linda Mar Boulevard. Francisco Sanchez, proprietor of the almost nine-thousand-acre Rancho San Pedro, finished this historic adobe in 1846. Several huge Monterey Pines and cypresses near the adobe have survived. Sanchez was the son of a commander of San Francisco's Presidio, a militia captain, and repeatedly an *alcalde* (magistrate) of San Francisco. The building, constructed of adobe bricks from an earlier mission outpost (now marked by a wooden cross), was beautifully furnished and the scene of many brilliant social events. After Sanchez died in 1862, the structure had a checkered career as a roadhouse, a speakeasy (and possibly worse), and then a shed for arti-

choke packing. The building itself has been artfully restored. Few of the furnishings are from the rancho period, but a move is on to replace them with items from that era.

When Proposition 13 was passed, cutting back State of California expenditures, the Sanchez Adobe had to be closed. A foundation came to the rescue, however, and the adobe is now open Tuesday and Sunday from 1 to 5, with a coordinator on hand to give information and help. Groups wishing to see the historical building on other days can call 415/359-1462.

A short distance farther along on Linda Mar Boulevard is the entrance to Pacifica's new *San Pedro Valley County Park*, open 8 A.M. to dark. A small brochure describes the park as consisting of "hills and small flat areas." There are also

San Pedro Valley County Park

trees and two creeks, and the park is often sunny when the coastal area a mile away is blanketed by fog. So if chill fog has driven you away from the oceanside you might use the picnic tables here. Another advantage: there are clean public restrooms, which you will discover are much in demand along the coast. Hopeful plans call for hiking and riding trails set up in loops, with several vista points, paralleling the middle fork of San Pedro Creek that flows through the area. The hikes would be set up for one hour to one day's duration. Already there are a gentle trail for the handicapped and a moderate hike for those who wish to see the waterfall when nature lets it operate.

Frontier Park

To the left near the entrance of this big park is the small *Frontier Park,* which has barbecue pits and a children's playground. Also to the left is the site of St. Peter's Catholic Church, frequently admired for its nontraditional, carousel architectural form. But the church is no more. The roof sagged so badly that the building had to be torn down. Only a few timbers are left among the weeds.

The *Linda Mar Shopping Center,* where Linda Mar meets Highway 1, is not photogenic, but it is attractive if you need gas, beer, sunburn lotion, or whatever to ease your travel. An oasis in this asphalt is

Periwinkle art supplies

the *Periwinkle Art Supplies and Framing Shop,* a delightful place to browse and chat with Enid Emde, the ebullient manager. She is knowledgeable about local political and cultural activities and, of course, local artists and art.

Pedro Point is worth a look. Take San Pedro Road past the Safeway store toward the point; turn right on Danmann. Ahead, at the end, you'll see one of the few remaining stations of the ill-fated Ocean Shore Railroad, this one now a private dwelling.

Pedro Point

Unfortunately for present-day adventurers, Danmann's Hayloft, a neighborhood bar dating from 1904, burned down a decade ago. A visit here was not for the fainthearted. Drinks were stiff and conversation ranged from gamey to near-violent.

The edifice on the right with the tower is now called the Arts and Heritage Building; activities held there range from frequent jazz concerts on Sunday to classes in dance, calligraphy, yoga, art and programs for children. Call 415/359-5230 to find out what's going on.

Across the street is a surfing shop and the Sea Urchin Gallery, which has a big collection of seashells.

Shelter Cove at Pedro Point

Shelter Cove, a private beach, is at the end of a narrow, often muddy private road that branches off to the left at the end of Danmann Avenue. About fifty people, including artists and a botanist, live here facing the raw Pacific. "On a warm sunny day, it's the most beautiful place in the world," a resident said, "but when it's rainy the sand turns into mud, and when it's stormy—watch out." Waves often crash over the seawall; once one picked up a van and threw it onto a porch. Yet these Shelter Cove inhabitants consider themselves lucky to have a front-row seat to the drama of the sea and to watch, close-up, great gray whales scraping against the rocks at Pedro Point to rid themselves of barnacles.

Residents can also enjoy the year-round display of wildflowers; the fog helps keep the plants blooming throughout summer.

As for trying to snare seafood, you can indulge in crabbing and almost any variety of fishing at Pedro Point. This is excellent rock-fishing and skindiving country. Authorities who keep count of catches insist that other fishing methods are more likely to bring in fish, but to a skindiving addict, perhaps it doesn't matter.

fishing from a boat
If you can, wangle yourself into a skiff or small boat here, or if you have one use an inflatable rubber boat with an outboard motor. The latter are becoming popular along the coast because they require no trailer and you can easily inflate them with an electric pump connected to your car's cigarette lighter outlet. If you are in a boat you'll probably fish just beyond the breakers. Try for king salmon when they're running, though you'll probably have more luck bringing in blue rockfish, black rockfish, white croaker, ling cod, cabezon, jacksmelt, and kelp greening.

For maps and brochures extolling more Pacifica virtues, try the Pacifica Chamber of Commerce, 80 Eureka Square, Suite 117, Pacifica, CA 94044 (415/355-4122).

If you decide to forego Pacifica, continue on Highway 1. You'll swing around San Pedro Mountain past thick forests of eucalyptus trees originally imported from Australia over a century ago. Some people consider these shallow-rooted trees a nuisance because they drop debris and cut off

A wide sandy beach and a small shovel adds up to many happy hours for most youngsters.

views, but they are pungent and attractive to the passerby.

Soon the mountainside gets too steep for trees and you're at Devil's Slide, where Highway 1 hangs precariously, almost over the ocean.

motels
Three small motels have occasional vacancies, but reserve ahead. The three are *Marine View Motel*, 2040 Francisco Boulevard (415/355-2543); *Rockaway Motel*, Reina Del-Mar (415/355-9978); and *Seabreeze Motel*, 100 Rockaway Avenue, right on the ocean (415/359-3500).

RV parking
Self-contained RVs may be parked overnight at the city-run Pedro Beach. Check with the police (415/877-8612).

where to eat   If you're driving south from San Francisco and Daly City, continue on to Vallemar, although many locals eat at the modestly priced *Muffin Mine* in Eureka Square, near the Chamber of Commerce. Take the Paloma turnoff and turn east.

Romano's Restaurant (415/359-0528), the first restaurant you'll see as you drive into Rockaway Beach, has pizza and moderately priced full-course meals, which attracts large families. Decor is nostalgic Italian, with red-and-white checked tablecloths, candles in wine bottles thick with wax drippings, and waitresses in black silk. Rockaway Beach also contains the *Golden Lantern Cafe* (Chinese). At the *Acapulco* (Mexican food) the caliber varies from good to indifferent according to the cook's mood.

The three fancier restaurants right on the beach are all owned by Nick Gust. Frequent radio advertisements for them urge listeners to get away from it all, to come to the sea for a romantic tryst, cocktails, and perhaps even dinner. The *Moonraker* (415/359-0803), for the Trader Vic-type crowd, serves "gourmet dinners" Tuesday through Sunday, with a background of organ music. *Captain Charles* (415/359-6737), the first-floor restaurant, features, as you would expect, seafood.

Nick's Rockaway (415/359-3900), across the street, serves food at a wide range of prices. It's open every day from 10 A.M. to 2 A.M. There's organ music Wednesday through Sunday and a small orchestra for dancing on Friday and Saturday nights. Nick lights the ocean at night to make it all more romantic.

The most scenic hamburger stand along the coast must be the A & W overlooking the ocean just before the turnoff to Pedro Beach. As you munch your poppaburger or Coney dog, you can sit outside a few feet from the surf and watch dogs running happily along the beach and, farther out, surfers waiting for the big waves.

Perhaps when you turn into Pedro Point the *Vagabond Restaurant* will have changed hands and be open again. At this writing, its doors are closed.

The *Swallow Inn* (415/355-8245), in a square building farther along on San Pedro Road, is often crowded with locals who recommend its Szechuan and Hunan Chinese food. Be sure to reserve early.

From Devil's Slide to the Northern Edge of Half Moon Bay

(Montara, Moss Beach, El Granada, and Princeton-by-the-Sea)

3

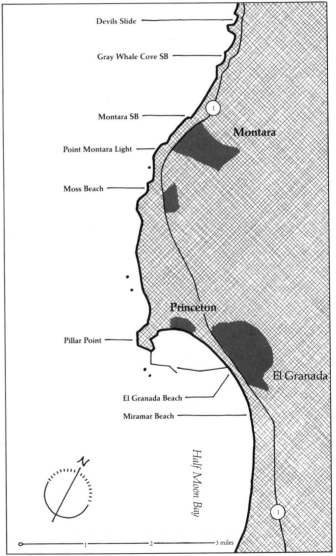

Devil's Slide

BETWEEN PEDRO POINT and Montara, Highway 1 turns into a cliffhanger above crashing surf. Steep cliffs, including the dangerous *Devil's Slide*, are just waiting to send rocks crashing down onto the highway. Drive slowly; the highway sags as much as fifteen feet at some points, and wrecks are almost commonplace.

In the spring of 1980, after months of heavy rainfall, old Devil's Slide again reverted to its evil ways, shoving a huge hunk of one lane of Highway 1 into the ocean almost a thousand feet below. Luckily no one was killed, but the inconvenience and economic hardship were considerable for those who depend on this vital route to get to and from the coastside. Only one lane could be used during the daytime while the highway was being patched up. Both lanes were finally opened for day and night use, but many folks are wondering what will happen if it rains heavily next winter or if there's an earthquake.

Because of the frequent slides, the twenty-six bad curves between Pacifica and Moss Beach, and the many accidents, years ago the Highway Department planned a Devil's Slide bypass. This wider freeway was to run inland, from .2 miles south of Pedro Creek in Pacifica to .7 miles south of San Vincente Creek near Moss Beach. The present scenic but dangerous portion was to be turned over to San Ma-

teo County, and it was expected that Devil's Slide would take over in the end. However, according to embittered local inhabitants, conservationists managed to block the bypass and the future of the new route is uncertain.

Devil's Slide is notorious as a popular dumping spot for bodies of murder victims. Some bodies plummet down the crumbling cliff into the surf; others don't and are discovered quickly.

When the ritual murder of a young man was reported, the *Half Moon Bay Review* commented that during Prohibition days, when bootlegging was rife, Devil's Slide was even more popular as a body dumping depot. Most of this activity resulted from gang fights and was rarely investigated, according to the newspaper.

On a clear day you can usually see the rocky Farallon Islands, more than twenty miles to the west. Be sure to avoid the steep paths down to the ocean right at Devil's Slide. The signs mean what they say: *Hazardous.* Swirling waters have trapped dozens of hikers here and many have lost their lives.

Another hazard, according to the Montara Fire Department, is the ever increasing number of gawkers who park illegally on the highway right of way, endangering themselves and others, while they peer below at the couples and families enjoying nude sunbathing at the three small beaches just south of Devil's Slide. *Gray Whale Cove State Beach*, the first, is now a state park with primitive restrooms. Parking is available for a stiff fee at a lot across Highway 1 from the beach, but you

Gray Whale Cove State Beach

The precarious Devil's Slide section of Highway One is closed periodically by rock slides.

have to cross the busy highway on foot. Gray Whale Cove State Beach is easy to get down to; the two tiny ones further south are only for the agile.

nude beaches   Back in 1979 the State Park Department announced public hearings on whether clothing should be optional at several state beaches. There was a loud outcry, led by Governor Brown, and the department backed down. The Half Moon Bay city council, frightened at the thought that nude sunbathing and roadside viewing might spread south from the Devil's Slide beaches, passed an ordinance banning sun worshippers-in-the-buff from the seven-mile stretch of beaches within the city limits. The fine is $50 for the first offense, and $500 and/or six months in jail for subsequent convictions.

As its name indicates, Gray Whale Cove State Beach is a good place to watch the giant gray whales as they migrate south at the end of November into February, returning in March and April. You can often spot them by their spout, or spume, a vapor they exhale before they dive. Several spouts in quick succession usually mean a long dive. You'll see them surface again at least a thousand feet farther along if you wait patiently with your binoculars for a few minutes.

The strange dirt and metal object looming up on a steep point just south of the three nudie beaches is the aborted view home of a Texan. He was in the process of having the old coast fortification there bulldozed down so he could build when the Coastal Zoning Act was passed. Afraid that he would never be allowed to build, he gave up and returned to Texas.

Montara State Beach

Coarse, sandy *Montara State Beach*, next south, drops off suddenly under water, which means (according to fishing experts) that surf casting is good. Rock fishing is okay, but rocks are scarce here.

Waves often churn and break wildly against this shore. A good place to watch is on top of the bluff to the south of the beach, where the late novelist Kathleen Norris had a family retreat.

Primitive restroom facilities and an easy entrance to the beach are available just south of the shingled Charter House restaurant, which replaced the once popular Frank Torres' seafood restaurant.

Point Montara Light Station

Farther south, just past a handful of private residences that flank Montara State Beach is the *Point Montara Light Station* (some of them aren't called lighthouses anymore). The stark, white buildings, with their red roofs against a background of dark-green cypresses, are a

The broad crescent of Montara Beach offers surf, sand, and views north toward Devil's Slide.

spectacular contrast to the crashing green surf and twisted, buff-colored coastline. This station has gone the way of many light stations. In the buoy a light and a sounding device operate automatically, as in the buoy installed on the Farallon Islands. Since the crew didn't have to tend the light and "fog howler," they were reassigned elsewhere and the buildings fell into disrepair.

Montara Youth Hostel

Then, starting in July, 1980, the once abandoned Montara Light Station took on new life as a youth hostel for the "young of heart of all ages." The state defines a hostel as a place for travelers to sleep, eat, wash, and make friends. As in other hostels, the guests provide their own food, sleeping bags, or linen, and are required to do some chores. Men and women hostelers usually bunk in separate dormitories, six to a room at Montara. The hostel is locked in the eve-

*Montara Light Station now offers accommodations
as a hostel for hikers and cyclists.*

ning for security. Drugs, alcohol, and guns are forbidden, and smoking is prohibited in bunkrooms or kitchens during meals. Television sets, radios, and other sound equipment can be used only at certain times in specified areas.

Hostels are certainly not for everyone, but the unusually dramatic location and the chance to meet fellow hostelers from all over the world (there are five thousand hostels in fifty countries) make the stringent rules and lack of luxury worthwhile for many.

The Montara Hostel is a twenty-five-mile bike ride from the big International Hostel in San Francisco's Fort Mason. It's the first unit of the State Park Hostel system, which will probably be turned over to the American Youth Hostel Association. Next, within biking distance of Montara,

is the Pigeon Point Lighthouse Hostel, south of Half Moon Bay. A hostel at Santa Cruz will complete a Bay Area hostel-hopping chain from Point Reyes in Sonoma County to Santa Cruz. The grand dream is to build a coastal hostel network from Canada to Mexico.

For more information or reservations, write the Montara Lighthouse Hostel, P.O. Box 737, Montara, CA 94037 or phone 415/728-7177.

Montara Ocean Shore Railroad Station

Drive by the *Montara Ocean Shore Railroad Station,* now a private home, before leaving Montara if you're a railroad buff. It's on the corner of Second Street and Main, a block inland from Highway 1. You can spot it by its two-foot-thick stone walls constructed with black mortar, sturdy enough to withstand the 1906 earthquake. The arched doorways and original beams remain. So does the former railroad platform, now a patio, with big red letters MONTARA in the concrete.

During those early days of the railroad, poet Joaquin Miller was invited to ride the first passenger train into Montara and plant a giant Sequoia tree there to inaugurate the expected growth of the town, which barely existed then. But the Sequoia tree died and—when the railroad tore out its rails in 1922—so did any hope for a booming town that might blossom into another Oakland.

Moss Beach

Moss Beach, 1.1 miles south of Montara, is famous for the tidepool life on its few miles of rocky sea shelf. Many sea creatures have their young in the protected nooks among the rocks. However, too many tidepoolers have walked away with specimens, and many species have almost disappeared. There are enough animals left, however, to be protected on San Mateo County's *James W. Fitzgerald Marine Reserve*, which may soon be included in the Golden Gate National Recreation Area. Take California Street seaward at a well-marked sign to the excellent parking area. You'll find restrooms and picnic tables under cypress trees, but no overnight camping.

James Fitzgerald Marine Reserve

Start your tidepool watching at a minus tide when the ocean has receded, so that rocks, seaweed, and sea life ordinarily covered by water are visible. A park naturalist, on duty from 8 A.M. to 5 P.M., will be glad to answer questions and can be persuaded to take groups on a lectured expedition at low tide. Since these walks often take place in the chill of early morning, you'll need to dress warmly.

The reserve has produced an excellent booklet describing local marine life. As you'll be seeing many of these same creatures along other beaches, here's a brief resume of some of the most common or most interesting.

tide pool life

In high and dry areas where the beach is exposed at about a two-foot tide you'll probably find periwinkles or a black turban snail, which will quickly withdraw into its shell, closing its horny door, if you pick it up. If you are patient you're also likely to see little hermit crabs scuttling about in the shells they've stolen for homes. You may even see a covetous home-seeker try to evict another hermit crab by pulling him out of his shell.

Farther out at low tide you'll find sea anemones. They might look merely like squishy, sand-covered lumps, but then again they might open up like flowers to show off the pink or white stinging tentacles with which they paralyze small prey, such as worms. Algae causes the vivid interior color of the giant green anemones, which can live for more than seventy-five years. The mossy chiton, a flat, oval animal with eight plates down its back, clings to the rocks and feeds on algae at night or at low tide. When the giant (up to a foot long) chiton dies, the shells that wash ashore look like petrified butterflies. Sea urchins, the spiny, purple porcupines of the sea, graze on seaweed. Limpets, small soft-bodied animals covered by conical shells, cling tightly to the rocks until nighttime or until the tide is in. Then they creep along on a muscular foot to feed on microscopic algae attached to the rocks.

Multilegged, clawed crabs scurry about in areas containing small rocks they can hide under. If the crab you see rears up and brandishes its pinchers to protect itself, it's a lined shore crab. If it's flat, with antennae, it's a porcelain crab. If it's large, with big claws and red spots on its belly, it's a red rock crab.

In surf-swept areas you'll find barnacles attached to the rocks with a glue twice as strong as any made by man. You may also see California mussels, their blue-black shells attached to the rocks with strong whiskerlike threads. You may also see the common ochre starfish—which is often red or purple—feeding by wrapping its rays (or arms) around a mussel and inserting its stomach into the mussel's shell.

seaweeds

Seaweeds are crucial to the tidal ecology, providing shelter for shellfish, fish, and sea mammals. Luckily, the names of many seaweeds suggest their appearance—for example, sea palms, which cling to surf-buffeted rocks; surf grass; Irish moss; sea lettuce; and feather boas. Bull whip kelp, a massive brown algae that can stretch more than fifty feet from the ocean floor to the surface, has air-filled flotation bulbs that pop when you step on them on the beach. Dulse looks like enormous flattened rubber gloves. Rock weed has olive-brown, flattened blades that exude a slimy mucilage to prevent drying.

To protect this fascinating tidal life, naturalists suggest that you always return rocks to their original position, remembering that seaweeds grow on the upper surface of rocks. Also, they stress, *do not remove any plants or animals or even rocks or empty shells.* These may be vital to the survival of some creatures in the pool. Besides, you'll want to leave them for others to enjoy.

sand dollars

On sandy beaches, you'll find only a few of the myriad species that live on rocky shores, but you will encounter "sand fleas." You may find some empty shells washed over from rocky points nearby, including sand dollars. Living sand dollars have hundreds of short, velvety legs. They live below the tideline in sheltered sand flats in bays or out beyond the force of the waves. The sand dollars you find will probably have lost these velvety legs and be bleached white. After they've dried out, break one gently and release the tiny dried objects inside, each scarcely larger than a grain of salt. Then decide whether these small objects look like doves of peace or tiny angels.

As you walk down the steps at the entrance to the Fitzgerald Marine Reserve, to your right on the cliff face a hundred feet north of the mouth of San Vincente Creek you can see the vertical trace of the Seal Cove earthquake fault. A sign nearby asks that you refrain from disturbing the cliff's face. A fault is a crack in the crust of the earth along which there is relative motion on each side. Here 7-million-year-old siltstone beds have moved up against the lighter, sandy terrace twenty thousand to seventy thousand years old. The spot draws geologists from all over the country, because it is one of the rare places where an earthquake fault zone can be viewed up close and in graphic detail.

rare earthquake fault

Eventually it is hoped that a two-mile coastline hiking trail will lead from the marine reserve along the bluffs, the beach, and over a ridge to Pillar Point. At present you can walk north along a trail in front of oceanfront homes. Your destination? The Montara sewer plant.

The Reefs

Near the entrance to the reserve, on the corner of Beach Street and Nevada, is Nyes Reefs II, a leftover from the days when Charles Nye ran The Reefs restaurant on a pier sticking out into the ocean. Nye entertained such luminaries as Jack London and Luther Burbank, but the ocean unkindly swept away The Reefs and the pier. At the present nearby rustic establishment, open sporadically on Saturdays and Sundays, you can drink beer and wine, and indulge in nostalgia as you play a funky jukebox.

Before you leave the area, drive along as close as you can to the ocean to see some of the old and contemporary houses and estates in this quiet community built within sound of the ocean. Also before you leave, visit the Moss Beach Distillery on Ocean Boulevard and Beach. This establishment replaced the Galway Inn, named because the restaurant overlooks a pleasant cove that is supposed to resemble Galway Bay in Ireland. Galway Inn took over from the old Vic Torres place, which prospered during the bootleg days, during the Prohibition era of 1919-1932. On the small hill nearby, lookouts would be stationed with lanterns to signal to smugglers in small boats offshore that all was safe and that they could bring in their cargo of Canadian whiskey.

the bootleg era

The whole Prohibition period is remembered as the Golden Era by many coastside oldtimers, who proudly relate how they smuggled bootleg whiskey in huge apron pockets or under coal or kept it behind revolving kitchen drawers. Business was rosy, not only for the boat smugglers and operators of stills back in the canyons, but for all their employees and hangers-on. Many of the tourists who flocked in for bootleg booze were also looking for a good meal and perhaps a little red-light activity, so lots of people were kept busy. When Prohibition was repealed, this somewhat lawless prosperity vanished, along with the excitement of playing tag with the "feds," and the accompanying gunfights and chases at sea.

From the old lookout hill near the distillery, take a good look at a small rocky island offshore. Especially at low tide, you may see harbor seals there. Even if you don't spot these shy sea mammals, however, the view from the windy bluff is worth tousled hair, especially at sunset or in spring when the banks are massed with wild iris.

Half Moon Bay Airport

The *Half Moon Bay Airport* is used mostly by small private planes (it's home to ninety, and there's an annual traffic of about eighty thousand planes), but medium-sized jets have landed here when the San Francisco Airport was socked in. You can sit in the small coffee shop and absorb some of the excitement of small-plane flying, or you can arrange for a half-hour plane trip over the coastline to San Francisco and back at a not-too-exhorbitant cost. Interested in flying lessons? On weekends an attractive woman schoolteacher is one of the instructors. In any case, you can't pick a much more beautiful area to fly over than the coastline around here, and there are several nude beaches to buzz.

candle seconds

The only industry in the vicinity seems to be candle making. You can stock up on inexpensive candle seconds at the *Blue Gate Candle Shop*, open for drop-in retail sales. It's on Airport Street, directly behind the airport and approached from Marine Boulevard on the north or from California Street.

On the inland side of Highway 1, just south of the airport entrance, a builder

Half Moon Bay Properties

named Doelger brought suburban living to what used to be an artichoke patch. Local parents, unhappy over the influx of new students in schools they contended were already overcrowded, picketed the tract in shifts, but the development sold out anyway.

Soon afterward, Doelger sold more than eight thousand acres to a Westinghouse affiliate, now called Half Moon Bay Properties. After putting up lush homes, the organization was caught in the rising tide of concern about keeping open space near the ocean, and many optimistic plans, including a nineteenth-century seaport village, have been curtailed or postponed.

Princeton-by-the-Sea

At present, the tourist's mecca, Princeton-by-the-Sea snuggles along the water south of the airport. The fishing boats bobbing in a harbor are protected on one side by a many-million-dollar breakwater, which will be increased, if plans materialize, along with more docking areas and harbor facilities.

Pillar Point

The harbor is also protected by *Pillar Point,* a spit of land that juts up and out at the end. Pillar Point is now treeless. However in 1585 when it was first sighted, Francisco de Gali reported, "we passed a very high and fair land with many trees, wholly without snow." Because of radar installations, some of the Pillar Point area is off limits, but you can enjoy marvelous views if you drive as far as possible on Ocean Boulevard in Princeton, park on the dirt area, and walk up to the edge of the cliff.

A collection of small art galleries and shops selling antiques, jewelry, and handi-

Princeton Wharf offers successful fisherman a convenient facility for cleaning their fresh catch.

crafts are strung out along Capistrano, Princeton's main street. However, by press time these modest enterprises may have disappeared, along with the Crab Shack, or have moved into a projected ten-unit building that will include other shops and two restaurants—all under the auspices of the Half Moon Bay Properties.

Right off Capistrano on Prospect is Pardini's, a small stand open Saturdays and Sundays, that vends fresh peas, artichokes, and other vegetables in season. A word to the wise about the fresh crab that's sold at some stands; it may be fresh-thawed crab, probably from Eureka.

The main attraction of Princeton, besides boating, is fishing: from the pier, from private boats, and from the big party boats that leave from the Pillar Point breakwater area at the south edge of

Princeton. According to Fish and Game experts, during 1979 in California nearly 775,000 anglers on party boats caught 6,647,227 fish. That's an average of better than 8.5 fish per capita, not a bad catch.

Party-boat fishing

Three firms operate party boats here. Captain John's (415/726-2913) has five boats, from 45 to 65 feet long. Those geared for bottom fishing leave early (six-ish) and a reservation is wise, especially on weekends or holidays. Captain John also has trips to the Farallon Islands to see the many sea mammals and sea birds. These are scheduled for Tuesday, Thursday, Friday, Saturday, and Sunday, and check-in time is at 5:30 A.M.

Pillar Point Fishing Trips (415/728-3377) has six boats that go out every day, all year, except on Thanksgiving and Christmas. On weekends the boats depart at 7 A.M. and return at 2:30 P.M.; on weekends they leave at 6:30 A.M. This company also has trips to the Farallon Islands every day except Tuesday and Wednesday, and you can buy breakfast and lunch on the boat. There are other trips, including special ones for whalewatching, birdwatching, and burial at sea. On the long-range and overnight sportfishing excursions, boats may go out forty to a hundred miles after albacore or night fish for swordfish and salmon if they are running. Pillar Point's Pacific Wilderness nature trips, for watching the sea otters, loop from the Farallon Islands to Point Reyes to San Francisco's Seal Rocks to Carmel. In the works is a plan for ten-day excursions to Scammon's Lagoon in Baja California, to see the gray whale in its mating grounds.

The Huck Finn II is a newcomer. (415/728-5677)

The fee for local fishing trips is somewhat lower than in San Francisco. Prices do not include fishing equipment, bait, sinkers, sacks for your catch, or fishing licenses (available there at additional cost). Nor do they include such necessities as beer, seasick pills (take them half an hour before embarking), a warm windbreaker, a knife, or lunch.

The boats on the short-range trips chug back and dock at around 2:30, when an audience watches the passengers disembark—usually with gunny sacks loaded with bottom fish such as rock cod, bass, red snapper, ling cod, and so on, but rarely salmon. Professional fish cleaners show up to clean and fillet the fish for a slight additional fee.

Sometimes amazing coincidences occur, for example, the time three eager Fish and Game officials were waiting at the dock for a party boat to dock. Not one of the eight fishermen who had not bothered to take out fishing licenses had caught a single fish.

Alongside Captain John's and the Pillar Point Fishing Company is the Princeton Seafood Company with a live seafood tank and a small establishment that sells beer, coffee, and snacks, from chowder to hamburgers. At the Abalone Shop you can find almost anything in season, from huge sea urchins to swordfish to salmon to freshly thawed lobster, but take out a bank loan first if you're planning to buy in quantity. The owner of the Abalone Shop is Bill LaVey; he's the man with the big mustache

Fishermen wet their lines at Princeton Wharf against a backdrop of boats riding at anchor.

wearing rubber boots and apron. On weekends from noon to five you can often watch Luana Ige demonstrate fish cookery and make up walk-away seafood cocktails, plus Japanese sashimi and sushi.

recipes for less expensive fish

Both Luana and LaVey will describe ways to prepare the less popular and, therefore, much cheaper fish and shellfish. (See mussel recipe on page 22.) Shark fillets, for instance, are great charcoal broiled after they've been brushed with an oil and vinegar salad dressing, and they're also good baked with cream of mushroom

Shark

soup in a covered pan at 350 degrees until the fish flakes. Besides being dense and delicious, there are no bones in shark to contend with; their skeletons are cartilage or gristle. Chunks of cabezon, a fish as ugly as it is inexpensive, can be simmered in a crock pot along with potatoes, tomatoes, onions, and any other vegetables, such as carrots, that you usually add to stews.

The roe of sea urchin, a prized deli-

sea urchin roe cacy in Japan, is slowly becoming more popular in California. The roe actually consists of the gonads (sex organs) of both males and females; each sea urchin has five. After the shell is split open with a knife, the gonads, which look something like oval gobs of tapioca pudding, are carefully lifted out and rinsed off. To be palatable they should be yellow or orange or occasionally pink. There's no further preparation. You eat them—gulp—raw.

barnacles— mock lobster Even gooseneck barnacles can be good to eat, comparable in taste and texture, some enthusiasts say, to lobster. The 24 July 1916 issue of *California Fish and Game* gives these directions. Wash the barnacles in the shell thoroughly with a small brush; then put them in a colander to dry. Boil in strong salt water until the barnacles shrink free from the shell and remove the heavy skin from the necks. The barnacles may then be prepared in a salad or made into hors d'oeuvres. For the latter, season the barnacles with butter, a little parsley, and a pinch of garlic; cover and steam for a few minutes; then add lime or lemon juice and serve on a hot plate.

The Princeton breakwater area also boasts a place to launch boats, free public restrooms, and a sizeable parking area adjacent to Highway 1. Self-contained RVs can stay overnight for a modest fee, but the reason the fee is modest is that facilities are primitive.

pier fishing Very important are the two long fishing jetties where families can try pier fishing. On the west jetty (nearest Pillar Point) fishing buffs bring in kelp fish, greenling, striped sea perch, and other species usually found near rocks. White croakers, surf perch, and flatfish are caught mainly from the east jetty. (See section on pier fishing on page 27.) Pillar Point is also popular with skindivers, and surfers show up in huge coveys at gently sloping El Granada Beach, next south.

Besides all these sports, because of the small swells and the winds averaging between 10 and 20 knots, Pillar Point is ideal for another comparatively new sport, **wind surfing** windsurfing. Usually out beyond the breakwater, the windsurfer rides something like a long surfboard outfitted with a mast and 52 square feet of sail. Windsurfers can skim along at 20 knots, and when turning, sometimes lean almost into the water. This sport is exciting and even dangerous, so experts advise learning the skills in protected waters. The city of San Mateo offers summer windsailing classes (415/574-6730, extension 87).

El Granada and Miramar beaches The next beach south of the jetty is El Granada Beach, which runs into *Miramar Beach*, which blends into a series of state beaches. Since there are no rock hazards at El Granada and Miramar beaches, you can enjoy the safest swimming available north of Santa Cruz. You can enjoy swimming, that is, if you can stand the chill water, usually in the low fifties.

That long stretch of sandy shore also attracts hikers and/or beachcombers. If they keep an eye on the surf and wait for a low tide, they can walk along three miles of uninterrupted beach from the Pillar Point breakwater to the end of the Miramontes Point Road, at the southern boundary of Half Moon Bay.

El Granada

Residences in the town of El Granada spill down slopes east of the highway, and are partially hidden by trees. Just off the highway is another old Ocean Shore Railroad depot. It now houses the Lane Realty Company, but about all visible that's left from the original depot is the red tile roof.

Miramar

Much of *Miramar* is inside the Half Moon Bay city limits. The Miramar Beach Inn (415/726-9053), highly visible from Highway 1, is at Magellan and Mirada Road. Besides dining by the sea it promises dancing daily from 9:30 P.M. and Sunday afternoons to bands with such names as Fastball, Hoodoos, Hooker, Sass, and the like. Those who prefer quiet can come for lunch or dinner and leave before the music takes off.

Bach Dancing and Dynamite Society, Inc.

Another musical get-together spot is the nearby *Bach Dancing and Dynamite Society, Inc.* (415/726-4143). Why drive to Monterey for your day by the sea? asks the society, pointing out that they're only thirty-five minutes' driving time from the outskirts of San Francisco or Palo Alto. On Sunday afternoons, usually at 4:30, jazz artists from saxophonists to vocalists to guitarists to combos show off their abilities. The audience, which is allowed in at 3:00 P.M., to save seats, can enjoy the program as they gaze out towards the ocean, sip the wine, and munch on the food they have brought.

The society was incorporated in jest in 1964 after jazz musicians had been coming to the beach to jam informally in an intimate and noncommercial situation. Since then it has expanded to include most other brands of music, classical to folk. Now on

The Village Green at El Granada purveys the food and ambience of Merrye Olde England.

most Fridays there's a catered dinner by candlelight at 7 P.M. followed by a classical concert at 9. You're expected to bring your own wine and a healthy contribution.

A short distance south on Mirada Road, just before the road tumbles into the ocean, is one of the coastside's most unique structures, straight out of *Hansel and Gretel.* It's the *New Age Center,* also known as the Miramar Beach Health Club, designed by Michael Powers, a photographer turned sculptor. Powers and helpers built

New Age Center

The eclectic New Age Center at Miramar is the studio-home of coast photographer Michael Powers.

it completely of wood from nearby forests and recycled salvage materials. The main building, a five-pointed star, supports a huge carved angel on top plus three lesser carved female figures. A huge piece of red-wood derricked in from the beach was placed in the center of the outside/inside area. A hexagonal building in the rear is leased to a holistic dentist. Michael has his bed, desk, and telephone in a beached boat within listening distance of the surf. Eventually plans call for the cluster of buildings and a garden to be covered by glass, a la a

solarium. As with the Douglas beach house, which houses the Bach Dancing and Dynamite Society, Powers will rent out his center to interested groups (415/726-2748).

beach erosion

The condition of the Mirada Road is mute testimony to what happens when man imposes on nature. In the years since the nearby Princeton breakwater was built, Miramar's beach has been disappearing. Usually, sand drifts out in winter and returns in the summer. Now not enough sand returns to the beach below the road; many feel it is trapped by the breakwater. Now the sea laps right up to the cliff under the road, and even though huge rocks have been placed along the ocean's edge, Mirada Road still crumbles away.

When you can't drive any farther, turn left and return to Highway 1. Immediately you're in Half Moon Bay.

where to stay

Self-contained RVs can be parked overnight on the parking area above the Princeton breakwater for a modest fee. The adventurous and young at heart can share six-person dormitories at the Montara Lighthouse Hostel. Otherwise—zero.

where to eat

The area is rife with eating establishments. A few are excellent.

In Montara, *Charter House* (415/726-7366), immediately south of Devil's Slide, is part of a chain. The food is not inexpensive, but the unusual structure and view are four-star. Diners in the know suggest that the very hungry really stoke up at the salad bar.

Dan's, in Moss Beach, is an old Italian family place at Etheldore and Virginia

Avenue (415/728-3343). Many oldtimers eat there.

Also in Moss Beach is *Tillie's "Lil" Frankfurt* (415/728-5744), at 2385 San Carlos Avenue, just across from the entrance to the Marine Reserve. Try it for a change of pace. The food is bounteous and modestly priced and there may be a seasoning of excitement when Tillie, who actually is from Frankfurt, rolls up her sleeves to take on someone out of line. Wednesday is family night, with a hearty entree, wine, and dessert. Sunday brunch is served from 8:30 to 12:30ish.

The Moss Beach Distillery Restaurant (415/728-5434), closed Wednesdays, has changed hands, menus, and lifestyles many times in the decades since the Vic Torres Golden Era of bootlegging. The view of the Bay remains superb. The restaurant presently offers lunch and weekend brunch and has a salad bar and oyster bar. Turn right at the big sign and continue to the beach and ocean. It's hoped that you're not in a hurry.

In Princeton, a few restaurants serve chowder, fish and chips, and so on. *The Princeton Inn* (415/728-7311), on Capistrano, is now a National Heritage building. It, too, has changed hands frequently. At last report the new regime was catching on for lunch, dinner, and Sunday brunch.

The Shore Bird (415/728-5541) is a popular Princeton eatery. It's so popular, in fact, that a big addition was built recently. The lunch crowd leaves around 4 P.M., the dinner contingent arrives about 5ish. Prices for steak, lobster or seafood are not out of reach. The catch of the day is often the best bargain (also, don't pass up shark). Touches include homemade salad dressing, hot sourdough bread, and a rose when you leave. Bonuses: the help is friendly, the atmosphere charming, and there's a small outside patio for sunny days.

Princeton's *Ida's* (415/726-2822) has earned renown for its abalone, although prices for this seafood delicacy are now in orbit. Ida's is just south of the Pillar Point breakwater right off Highway 1, and it has a view of the harbor.

The Moon Garden is next door to Ida's. If seafood isn't your forte, you can eat Mandarin Chinese food here.

In El Granada, *The Village Green* (415/726-3690) is at 89 Portola Avenue, across from the post office. It purveys authentic English farmhouse-type breakfasts, lunches, and teas, which include homemade scones and pastries, or cucumber sandwiches, or bangers. The ambience is strictly English. Teas are correctly served in pots wearing tea cozies, but nothing is perfect—the china is from Japan. The restaurant is run by two genuine Englishwomen. Marilyn Haslett is an ex-secretary from near London. Susan Hayward, who doubles as a ballet teacher, was originally from Bath. After bravely starting the restaurant in 1968, the two learned as they went along. Their most important lesson? It's hard work to run a restaurant, especially when you do your own baking. During the winter season, the last Sunday of each month is Pub Night, when guests and an invited cockney sing pub songs together.

Half Moon Bay

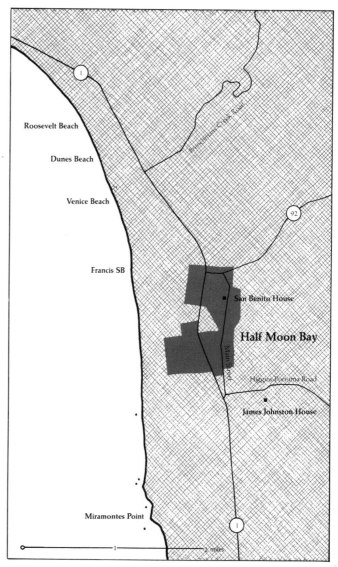

HALF MOON BAY proper, the largest town on the coastside, has an official population of only 7500. But on a summer or fall weekend, you may assume that several times that number live here, though the balance are probably mostly visitors from "over the hill." According to one authority, tourists have replaced vegetables as the number two crop along the coastside. The flower industry is still number one.

beaches

Most of the visitors are bound for picnicking, beachcombing, or surf fishing on the four miles of sandy beaches that rim the bay. On some beaches you can surf net, too. If you're driving south on Highway 1, the first two beaches just south of Miramar can be reached via Young Avenue. At *Roosevelt Beach* 70 cars can park on dirt. *Dunes Beach* can handle 150 cars on a gravel parking lot. Both have flush toilets and there's drinkable water at Dunes. The next beach south, *Sweetwood*, has a group camp area and room for eight cars. You can reach *Venice Beach* via Venice Boulevard. It has a 50-car gravel parking lot and restrooms.

Francis State Beach

The biggest and most popular beach is *Francis State Beach* at the end of Kelly Avenue; turn at the light. Francis charges an overnight fee of $5.00 nightly whether you plan to park a self-contained RV, pitch a tent, or just put your sleeping bag out under the foggy night sky. If you're a hiker or arrive on a bicycle, however, this is one of the campgrounds along the Bikecentennial Highway 1 route that lets you roll out your sleeping bag for only 50¢ a night.

Day use costs $2.00 per car. You get a lot for your money: paved parking for 240 cars, a 50-unit campground, picnic and firepit facilities, a sanitation dump station, and three restrooms. Beach access is easy, too.

For more information or reservations on these or any of the state beaches from Thornton Beach at the northern boundary of San Mateo County to Año Nuevo State Reserve near the Santa Cruz County line, call 415/726-6238. Park headquarters, open Monday through Friday from 8 A.M. to 4:30 P.M., are at the end of Kelly Avenue. If you're sixty-two or over, say so when you reserve and get a 50 percent reduction.

Sierra Club hike

Among hikes listed by the Sierra Club Peninsula Regional Group is a jaunt from Francis State Beach to Eel Rock, five miles south. The description warns that you have to clamber over a bluff at one point and advises that you take the hike at low tide. If you would like more information on many more hikes and activities in the area, contact the Loma Prieta Chapter of the Sierra Club, 2253 Park Boulevard, Palo Alto, CA 94306, or call 415/327-8111 Monday through Friday from 1 to 5.

golf

But back to Highway 1. Just south of Miramar across from a driving range (415/726-9874) is *Corbin's Art Gallery*, open weekends only. Every item in this gallery has been made by Dale Corbin, his wife

Anna, his daughter, or sister-in-law. The Corbins specialize in paintings, small sculptures, oversized chess sets, and totem poles. The totem poles and totem head-boards for beds are made to order in red-wood or cedar. The Corbins put in many years studying Indian lore to give their handicraft an authentic look.

roadside stands   Next south is the first of several fruit stands that feature freshly picked arti-chokes and dried artichoke blossoms, which make lovely permanent arrange-ments. Several other roadside stands are located farther inland on Highway 92. Some farms that sell fresh produce in the area (you'll see their signs on the highway when the crops are ready) tell you their produce is fresher because it is under a roof and has not been exposed to the sun all day.

artichokes   Italians and other artichoke converts insist that this member of the thistle family is nutritious, full of vitamins, and deli-cious, and you're sure to meet its fleshy flowers on some menu here or in San Fran-cisco. If you're new to California, don't be ashamed if you don't know how to eat them. Usually you tear off a leaf, dip the large end in mayonnaise or hot butter, and strip off the tender green portions between your teeth. Under the fuzzy choke, which you throw away, is the even more tender heart.

To prepare artichokes, pull off the lower outer leaves, cut the stem to one inch, and snap off the tips of remaining leaves. Stand them up in a pot in three inches of water; add ¼ teaspoon regular or garlic salt per artichoke. Some cooks top each artichoke with olive oil or butter and lemon juice. Cover and boil the chokes gently for thirty-five minutes or until a fork pierces the base easily. Some of the artichoke growers themselves prefer the tiny artichokes, which are usually much less expensive and are so tender they can be cut in two and added to stews, for in-stance, without all the preparation the larger chokes require.

pumpkins   Arichokes and pumpkins are practi-cally a religion along the coastside, and the biggest and most highly advertised pump-kin stand is *Tom and Pete's,* just off High-way 1, Main Street and 92. John Minaidis, Sr., the owner, is credited with starting the coastside pumpkin boom (more about the pumpkin festival later). Now, besides those turned over in his whopping whole-sale trade, Minaidis sells more than fifty thousand pumpkins a year. Every October busloads of children visit his colorful acreage and marvel; some of the pumpkins grow to three hundred pounds.

horses   Sandy beaches and pumpkins aren't the only tourist lures. Horseback riding, horse boarding, and rodeos have become increasingly popular. You can rent horses at Friendly Acres (415/726-9871), on the leeward side of the highway just past the entrance to Dunes Beach. Sea Horse Ranch, farther south, also rents horses and arranges for hay rides (415/726-2362). Al-though horseback riding is not permitted on state beaches, a series of trails for eques-trians runs behind the Half Moon Bay beaches parallel to the ocean frontage, and many riders head for a non-state-owned beach just south of Francis State Beach.

Frenchman's Creek

Across the highway, the *Frenchman's Creek Road* heads back toward the hills, through fields of cultivated flowers and fields of upper-bracket homes put up by developers.

Frenchman's Creek was named for a legendary encounter between a Frenchman hunting beaver and a grizzly bear. History doesn't report who won, so take your pick.

Galen Wolf

The late Galen Wolf, a well-loved coastside artist whose paintings are still being shown at the Spanishtown Art Gallery on Highway 92, lived near the end of the Frenchman's Creek Road. His uncle bought hundreds of acres in this sunny pocket from Bernal, an original Spanish land grantee, and leased out some of the land for flower growing. Wolf, active to the last, hated "ticky-tack." When he first moved to Half Moon Bay he used to tell visitors, "he painted clean rocks, clear beaches and untouched hills covered with warm, golden grass." Doves nested in alders behind his house and two mountain lions, one a 220-pounder, were shot on his property. "Then many birds and animals fled, and the beaches and streams were no longer clear."

wildflowers

But not all natural beauty has fled the coastside. In winter the hills are still green with grass, in summer they're burnished with yellow-gold, in spring the orange-gold poppies (California's official flower) put on a show, and all year long the miles of flowers around Half Moon Bay are a delight.

cultivated flowers

Even before you reach the outskirts of Half Moon Bay you'll notice huge wholesale nurseries; the growing of cultivated flowers accounts for many millions of dollars a year along the coastside. As you're driving along Highway 1, perhaps you'll see acres ablaze with lilies, heather, or helichrysum, which can be turned into straw flowers. (There's a straw flower factory in Pescadero and several gift shops sell the products.) Or perhaps as you round a curve on Highway 92 you'll see workers waist deep in fields of sunlit daisies. Many of these flowers end up far afield with florists in other cities; some, of course, brighten San Francisco's famous flower stalls.

However, enjoy the acres-wide flower exhibit only from the highway. Visitors are not welcome at big wholesale nurseries because dangerous machinery and lethal sprays are about. A few small retail nurseries are sprinkled along Highway 1; a large one, the Half Moon Bay Nursery, is inland on Highway 92, and you can buy some of the cut flowers and ferns at several roadside stands.

Half Moon Bay's name

Half Moon Bay was named after that four-mile crescent of sandy beaches. Originally the town was known as *San Benito.* Then it was a cluster of adobes belonging to families who owned two big, adjoining Spanish land grants. More Spanish-speaking people drifted in, and the few Americans who arrived dubbed it *Spanishtown.* Next came clans of Portuguese. Even today many storekeepers find it helpful to know English, Spanish, and Portuguese.

Although its boundaries extend about five miles south from the edge of Miramar, Half Moon Bay's population of 7500 is small for an area so close to the crowded

Peninsula and San Francisco. Even if you add the population of outer Half Moon Bay, from Montara south to San Gregorio, you'll come up with only about 12,000 official inhabitants.

At one time rumors flew of new industries coming, one manufacturing educational computers and eventually hiring over a thousand employees. But the area still hasn't licked its transportation problem. If the freeway from the Peninsula to Half Moon Bay is finished and a freeway built that will bypass Devil's Slide, the coastside will explode for better or worse. If you're a land developer or a city father looking for added taxes, it may be for the better. If you're a taxpayer, providing schools, sewage, police and other services to newcomers, the expansion might be a headache. And if you've moved to the area because it is relatively uncrowded or if you're a conservationist who believes in green belts and open space, the projected growth would be all for the worse. The battle is on, and reading the reports in the weekly *Half Moon Bay Review* is exciting.

oil drilling   Added to local tensions, there's a possibility that oil rigs will be permitted along this coast. Concerned groups and citizens, including the California Coastal Commission and the San Mateo County Board of Supervisors oppose drilling along this "sensitive and treasured" coast. The project was dropped, then reactivated. Its future depends on which way the political winds blow.

shopping centers   Even with the transportation, sewage, and water problems, population of the greater Half Moon Bay area has increased slowly but inexorably. As families flee from cities "over the hill" to the ocean-washed air, new businesses have followed, mostly clustered in shopping centers. The big, conspicuous center, with the Alpha Beta supermarket, service stations, chain drugstore, and sandwich shops, marks the junction of highways 1 and 92. Among the many establishments in this busy shopping center is Blanda's, a small haven of gourmet cheeses, lunch meats, and soup. You can order "to go" or eat it here.

One hundred years after Levy Brothers first established a store in Half Moon Bay, and about sixty-six years after the store moved inland to San Mateo, the firm has returned to Half Moon Bay at this same shopping center. In 1872, when it opened, Levy Brothers sold mostly general merchandise—everything from hay, grain, and feed to furniture and root beer. Their stage coach carried mail and passengers to San Mateo in three hours; present mail, some natives say, now takes up to two days. Levy Brothers' telegraph station flashed orders to San Francisco, where fast teams or steam vessels brought merchandise to the coast within thirty hours. Now *Levy Brothers'* "new" Half Moon Bay Store emphasizes clothing for the family.

Farther east the big Ocean Shore Hardware Store, a fabric shop, and garden shop have sprouted. Less visible, north and on the seaward side, at the Strawflower Shopping Center, you can eat, buy country clothes, art, real estate, and have your hair coiffed, and "arty" establishments are spreading into town.

If Main Street looks more quaintly

colorful than the last time you drove through, it's due to a general face-lifting and historical restoration. A Main Street Beautification Committee voted in late 1970 to go ahead with plans for a general painting and restoration of most of Main Street. Consultants were hired to draw up the overall plans. On a sunny weekend in May local townspeople did the actual painting, planting trees and flowers and changing signs. Oldtimers, long-haired youths, and folks of every age between clambered over scaffolds with paint-brushes while others played music or prepared food for the paint crews. One result, at least, was the reluctant admiration admitted to by some of the local Establishment after working alongside many bearded hippies.

As the years passed, more trees and flowers were planted, street lamps made to look like the original gas lamps appeared, and more buildings, especially the professional ones, were Victorianized. Inevitably the town's new look attracted more tourists. Not everyone approved, since inevitably, too, rents increased. One antique dealer, driven out by a rent increase, warned that Half Moon Bay was in danger of becoming "Carmelized." She reported that whenever an oldtimer living on Main Street dies, the home becomes a shop to lure tourists. The big Shoreline Station complex has three buildings of shops, the remodeled Alves House contains eight "shoppes," and there are other little pockets of tourist shops along Kelly.

Main Street at present is a mixture of old and new. Soon after you leave High-way 92 and cross the funky concrete bridge (circa 1900) you'll see the Half Moon Bay Feed and Fuel Store on your left. It not only smells of hay and wood but also carries almost everything a local farmer or horseman might want, from fly swatters to Greek purses to hand plows. The store is also unofficial headquarters for exchanging, buying, or selling rabbits, horses, and other livestock.

Main Street stores

A newcomer (spring of 1980) is the Buffalo Shirt Company, (415/726-3194), at 325 Main, run by pleasant Bob "Buffalo" MacCall and his wife, Isabelle, an airline stewardess. The couple decided that Half Moon Bay was preferable to San Francisco as a commute from the San Francisco Airport. Here life was more leisurely and you could still breathe fresh air. The shop sells shirts, but also big canvas bags, brass objects, local "Sonshine Pottery," washable hand-knitted sweaters from Portugal, and more.

Next door is a yarn shop and around the corner a travel service that also sells gifts and gadgets.

At the corner of Main and Mill streets is another of the Half Moon Bay buildings that has been tastefully restored, this to a mid-nineteenth-century ambience. It's the San Benito House and Saloon, formerly Dominic's, and before that the Mosconi Hotel. Four local people joined together to give the drab building a facelift. Layers of old paint were stripped, and new paint was added, along with flower boxes. Eventually chef/owner Carol Regan hopes the building will be smothered in bougainvillea. Brass chandeliers now decorate the

San Benito House

San Benito House at Half Moon Bay offers accommodations by reservation and a very pleasant dining room.

high ceilings of the dining room and French doors open onto a garden with graveled walks where guests can eat lunch on sunny days.

Upstairs, the San Benito House is in the tradition of old country inns. The ten rooms are somewhat spartan and occasionally noisy, but there are extra touches like bathtubs big enough for two, fresh flowers, and fluffy comforters. Guests can also relax in a nonhistoric sauna bath or on a flower-bedecked back porch, where they can absorb sun, if any, and chat with each other. Carol says that guests may also use

her busy kitchen as a home away from home (415/726-3425).

At present the saloon seems to be a gathering place for local workmen, each clutching a beer bottle as he watches sports on the TV set. The restaurant crowd is quieter, and the men usually wear jackets.

There's a bicyclery in the next block, plus an auto parts store and the Half Moon Bay Electric Company, at 420 Main. These places keep up with the tradition of many local establishments, flaunting and selling their own t-shirts, many with a pumpkin motif. The motto on the t-shirts sold by the electric company reads, "Let us remove your shorts."

Cunha's Country Grocery

The building housing Cunha's Country Grocery, at the corner of Main and Kelly, was once a general merchandise store and a saloon (one of eleven saloons in town at the time). Cunha's is stocked with fresh produce plus excellent wines, lunch meats, and cheeses, including an expensive but delicious goat cheese from the Azores. (No, it's not like Norwegian goat cheese.) In the upstairs area, which displays household items, you can buy the *Spanishtown Historical Society's Tour of the Half Moon Bay Area* for 25¢. The Nunes Meat Market, formerly next to the town bakery, has moved into the rear of Cunha's. The butchers here still sell old-fashioned custom cuts, if you prefer. At Sam's Mercantile, a block east at Kelly and Purisima you'll encounter a similar meat market, which also sells picnic supplies.

Historical-tour maps

One of the most popular establishments on Main Street is in the next block across from city hall. (If the city hall is

Half Moon Bay Bakery

open, you can obtain an excellent map of the Half Moon Bay area.) It's the *Half Moon Bay Bakery*, which still uses the original brick ovens; loaves are shoved into the oven on long wooden handles. Every day you can pick up freshly baked French bread here and, if you're lucky, delectable Portuguese sweet bread or focaccia, a delicious breadlike version of pizza. The bakery also sells sandwiches to go.

Next door, in the old I.O.O.F. Hall, is a relative newcomer, McCoffee's, open 10 A.M. to 6 P.M. seven days a week. Here you can buy gourmet kitchenware, sample the cheese of the week from among twenty varieties, buy imported cheesecake, and sip a cup of coffee freshly brewed from two or three exotic varieties. You can even bring in your pastry from the bakery and to nibble along with your coffee.

arts and crafts shops

Among other gift items, the Main Street Boutique and Gallery, at 521 Main, features ceramics by Sonia, a local artist. Some of her popular sellers are ceramic cats and pumpkins. The Yellow Brick Road, 523 Main, specializes in dollhouses and miniatures. Across the street Peggy Eriksen frames pictures and sells photographs of the area. Her consistent best sellers are mood pictures, such as boats in a fog, fence posts, or indistinct hillside views. George's Toggery, at 527 Main, is the oldest continuous business property in town. The only remaining hitching post stands outside the store.

In a big wooden building in the 700 block, the Boardwalk, run by Pat Dutra and Jean Byers, carries stationery, greeting cards—some in foreign languages—and a small selection of Portuguese blueware. Next door is a Western wear shop popular with urban cowboys.

Across the street is the Patchwork Pumpkin, a needlework and quilting emporium. Upstairs is a Christmas-All-Year corner. Other gift-type shops have moved in upstairs here, too.

If you prefer shopping at flea markets, try the *Saturday Thrift Shop* nearby—just south of Pete's at that sharp triangle where Main Street meets Purisima. Proceeds of sales go to help restore the historic Johnston House (see page 64). The volunteers who work here on the first two Saturdays of each month, most of them senior citizens, also appreciate donations of clothing or household items.

Nearer the Cabrillo Highway 1 are more establishments geared to tourists. The renovated *Alves House* (415/726-9926), 520 Kelly Avenue off Highway 1, is open Wednesday through Sunday from 11 A.M. to 6 P.M. Here you'll find antiques, a beauty shoppe, a store selling games including kites, one vending romantic apparel, one selling silk and dried flower arrangements, and others. Quilts West, on the first floor, carries, as you would expect, old and new quilts plus baby things.

Alves House

An even larger building, the *Shoreline Station*, across Kelly and just off Highway 1, contains almost forty shops and professional services. The Half Moon Bay Chamber of Commerce is now in the old refurbished railroad caboose, but you'll probably get more information about the area at city hall or Cunha's Country Grocery. The three buildings house galleries, a

Shoreline Station

The Queen Anne style Alves House at Half Moon Bay has been converted into this attractive shopping center.

Bay Book and Tobacco Company, a music center, a photo center, and a shop that sells collectibles.

The Holy Ghost Festival

The business section of Half Moon Bay comes to life in May—usually seven weeks after Easter—during the *Annual Holy Ghost and Pentecost Festival*, a colorful import from the Portuguese Azores. On Saturday night and again during a double-header on Sunday, you'll see dozens of reigning, future, and past festival queens and princesses, plus sizeable coteries for each. After the Saturday night procession, there's a feast and dance. On Sunday morning at about ten, the many queens plus marching bands parade down Main Street, turn at Kelly, and end up at Our Lady of the Pillar Church for Mass. The queens' costumes run to pastel, and just when you think you've seen the current queen, another group marches by. You can spot the newly crowned queen by her magnificent velvet train and by the heavy, ornate, silver crown made of melted silver dollars, which is carried by one of her huge coterie.

This fiesta (like the one that usually takes place a week earlier in Pescadero) originated centuries ago in the Azores. The legend is that when the people on one island were starving the Holy Spirit miraculously intervened and sent a foreign ship loaded with food. The ship's master fed the people and refused any pay; hence, the free barbecue now. Queen Isabella of Portugal herself led a procession through the streets to celebrate the delivery of her island people—thus the parade and the "royalty."

The Great Pumpkin Festival

Another celebration, which draws even bigger crowds, is the *Great Pumpkin Festival*, held the third weekend in October. On that Saturday local bands and hundreds of children dressed as witches, goblins, pumpkins, or whatever their parents have dreamed up, parade down Main Street. There's a pumpkin-carving and also a pumpkin eating contest for children, a pumpkin-decorating contest for everyone, a pumpkin recipe contest, plus a masquerade ball on Saturday night with prizes for best costumes. There's a haunted house to visit, plus several blocks of booths for food (which benefit local nonprofit organizations) and for arts and crafts. In 1980, the tenth anniversary, there were more than 210 arts and crafts booths plus 25 food booths run by locals. To avoid the often bumper-to-bumper traffic, check with SamTrans, which operates several tours (415/348-7325).

Each year the suspense grows as to who has produced the biggest pumpkins. Some reach three hundred pounds. Although Half Moon Bay considers itself the pumpkin capital of the world, outsiders from Ohio have been known to win the annual contest.

fair and rodeo

The newest event is the *Coastside Country Fair and Rodeo,* held during the Fourth of July weekend. It includes a horse show and parade, livestock displays, flower and vegetable exhibits, craft displays and a sand-castle-building contest.

gardens and buildings

While in the Half Moon Bay business area, spend a few minutes poking around back streets to look at occasional ancient cypress trees, the lush vegetable and flower gardens along the streets, even on Main Street, and the picturesque houses, some built more than a hundred years ago. One of the oldest houses in the area, built in 1869, once belonged to Pablo Vasquez, scion of an early Spanish family. It's at 270 Main Street, just north of the old reinforced-concrete bridge across Pilarcitos Creek. The first Vasquez home in Half Moon Bay, of adobe, was demolished to make way for the later house.

Artist Galen Wolf recalls in one of his historical rememberances the thrill of seeing Pablo Vasquez, "slender, grave, with white head and beard, unbelievably poised and graceful on his golden pony. Little hooves flicking like white butterflies, golden skin polished and glinting in the sun. They pass. An era passes on those twinkling hooves."

Many other interesting old buildings are sprinkled throughout this small town. A beautifully restored Greek revival house, once occupied by the Zabella family, is at 326 Main. The 25¢ walking-tour map, mentioned earlier, and put out by the *Spanishtown Historical Society,* P. O. Box 60, Half Moon Bay, CA 94019, covers more historical buildings than you'll probably have time to see.

historical walking tour

This map, also available at Cunha's Country Grocery, is well worth having, as Half Moon Bay has a lot of history going for it. Some Spanish names that evoke its historic rancho era still appear in coastside phone books; Gonzales, Castro, Sanchez, Vallejo, and Miramontes descendants still live in the Half Moon Bay area.

Here are a few highlights of the walking tour:

The *Community Methodist Episcopal Church,* at Johnston and Miramontes, is one of the oldest and most interesting Gothic Revival Protestant churches in San Mateo County; its social hall was once one of Half Moon Bay's *Ocean Shore Railroad Stations.*

An interesting Victorian house, built in the 1880s, with beehive shingling and colored-glass borders around the windows, is nearby at 505 San Benito Street at Kelly Avenue. The two-story building at the rear once housed a bakery.

A good example of nineteenth-century Victorian Gothic architecture is

the small, well-maintained house at 546 Purisima Street, a block west of Main Street.

At 520 Kelly Avenue, near an intersection with Highway 1, the large, lovely house with the scalloped shingling and polygonal tower of the Queen Anne period (after 1900) is now the Alves House, mentioned earlier. The small house next door was once used as a movie house.

The half-century-old *Our Lady of the Pillar Cemetery*, comparatively new as local cemeteries go, has an overall view of

The California winner at the 1980 Pumpkin Festival at Half Moon Bay was this king-sized 375-pound entry.

this essentially flat town, but you'll probably want to drive there. Go inland on Miramontes Street and take a sharp right immediately after crossing a small wooden bridge.

Unless you arrive by boat or helicopter or were born there, you can reach Half Moon Bay by two routes only: slow, two-lane Highway 1, which hugs the ocean, or

directions

The Community Methodist Episcopal Church, of the Gothic Revival style, is on the historical walking tour of Half Moon Bay.

Highway 92, a twisting, two-lane road. Five miles inland, 92 connects with even twistier Skyline Boulevard (Highway 35), and seven miles from Half Moon Bay with Highway 280, the six- to eight-lane freeway from San Francisco to San Jose.

Freeway 280   As freeways go, 280 is pleasant. Near the 92 turnoff it parallels *San Andreas Lake* and the *Crystal Spring Reservoir;* both follow the direction of the San Andreas fault, which was responsible for San Francisco's famous 1906 quake and fire. The area near the springs is a fish and game refuge popular with deer, and you may occasionally meet one that has leaped over the fence onto the freeway. Some morning commute broadcasts routinely report that a buck or doe is blocking one lane.

Kings Mountain, a tiny community six miles south of where Highway 92 joins Skyline Boulevard (Highway 35) puts on a big arts and craft fair every Labor Day weekend. Besides the many booths there are strolling musicians, paths among the redwoods, and spectacular views of Crystal Spring Reservoir and, on clear days, of San Francisco.   **Kings Mountain**

Spanishtown Center

What is there to see along Highway 92? On Fridays, Saturdays, and Sundays you can browse through the rustic *Spanishtown Arts, Crafts and Antique Center* (415/726-9971), where you might see artists and potters at work. Spanishtown, which opened in 1969, still attracts passersby, although more accessible collections of galleries and shops have opened in Half Moon Bay. The center was started to solve the perennial problems artists have in displaying their wares. Seven people set out to locate a place with low overhead where they could combine the advantages of a small shop with the atmosphere of a small studio. They finally decided that the best answer was to construct their own. The result is an unpretentious but charming building, inland about a mile from Half Moon Bay's Main Street.

The sign for Spanishtown promises "Art, Artisans, Artifacts and Antiques." Tiny shops sell stitchery, baskets, jewelry, wall hangings, boutique items, things for children, gifty planters, pottery, and so on. The big art gallery at the rear has a representative selection of paintings, sculpture, and pottery, with emphasis on well-known local artists. People with steady weekday jobs run most of the Spanishtown shops—juvenile probation officers and teachers in the majority—and it's hard to get away from them without succumbing to at least one purchase.

fresh produce and pumpkins

Artichokes, peas, pumpkins and fresh-cut flowers are also attractions along 92 when they're in season. (After Halloween you'll see cows busily munching the leftover pumpkins.) Several produce stands are open on the south side of Highway 92 during peak tourist periods. Among the signs along the way is one advertising well-diggers, "Digges and Son," plus several promoting tree farms where you can cut your own Christmas tree. As the holiday season nears you may be surprised to see Santa himself stroll out on the highway to entice you to his tree farm.

Christmas trees

One of the few coastside nurseries that welcomes visitors is farther inland—the *Half Moon Bay Nursery*. The proprietor, Ronald Mickelsen, is extremely knowledgeable about planting in the area and has a large and rare cactus collection.

House of Doors

You might find a glimpse at *Anne Howe's House of Doors* interesting. The house, actually made of doors from the San Francisco Exposition of 1915, is jammed against a steep hill, near a cascade of volcanic rocks, about two miles inland from Spanishtown on a dangerous turn on Highway 92. Keep a sharp lookout or you'll miss it.

A winery in Half Moon Bay? Recently many drivers who have rounded a slight curve about a mile east of Half Moon Bay have been surprised to see right off the highway a sign on the bottom of a wine cask: *Obester Winery*.

Obester Winery

Before the winery and small tasting room opened, Paul and Sandy Obester had lived near Paul's work—he had a high-powered electronics job in Palo Alto. Then, at the age of ninety, Sandy's grandfather sold out his Gelemmo's Winery in Mountain View and moved in with the Obesters. Still lively into his late nineties, he taught them the techniques of winemaking in the garage, and the Obesters became dedicated winemaking enthusiasts.

The result is their small winery and home by the side of the road overlooking a field of Marguerite daisies, where they can enjoy country life. However, running a winery and a tasting room is around-the-clock work, the Obesters have discovered, even with the help of their boys, David and Doug, and their dog, Angelica.

Since Half Moon Bay's climate is not optimum for grape growing, the Obesters travel to vineyards in Sonoma, Mendocino, Monterey and other counties. They walk through the vineyards row-by-row, selecting. The grapes they choose are picked in the early morning, crushed immediately, poured into a special portable tank, and brought to Half Moon Bay before the day heats up. There, according to the Obesters, the cool climate provides an ideal, energy-efficient environment for fermentation and oak aging. The Obesters have planted fifty experimental plants in Gewürztraminer, a grape purported to do well in cool, foggy climates, but they won't know the results for several more years.

Visitors can talk wine philosophy with the Obesters and sample their handful of wines—some already prize winners—any Friday, Saturday, or Sunday, and some holidays between 10 A.M. and 5 P.M. If you can't make it in then, call for a special appointment (415/726-WINE).

The *Hilltop Mobile Home Park*, 251 San Mateo Road, on top of a small hill, as its name implies, lies barely outside the main section of Half Moon Bay on 92. It is one of the few commercial places south of San Francisco where some trailers or campers can find space by the night or week. Check at the *Hilltop Store*, across the highway, where you can also buy groceries and fishing gear, and pick up tide tables early in the year.

Also on Highway 92, almost opposite the turnoff to Half Moon Bay, are the aging wood signs and the dark cypresses of the *Pilarcitos Cemetery*, established in 1820. The I.O.O.F. cemetery is behind it, and tombstones in both pioneer cemeteries bear mute evidence to the varied ethnic inheritance of the coastside.

Before leaving Half Moon Bay, for a glimpse of another of the old *Ocean Shore Railroad depots*, drive toward the ocean along Poplar Street under arching cypress trees to Railroad Avenue. The depot, now a private residence, is to your left. The deep eaves of the roof once projected over the railroad tracks, but the tracks are long gone.

Also, before leaving Half Moon Bay heading south, gas up if you're low. Service stations are sparse between here and Santa Cruz. Watch out for posted speed limits, too. Traffic fines are a popular way of filling Half Moon Bay city coffers.

For those who like quiet, bucolic scenery, the Higgins-Purisima Road, which starts where Main Street joins Highway 1, loops inland through rolling farmland and hillsides, returning five miles later to Highway 1.

The road passes Half Moon Bay's proudest historical site, the *James Johnston House*, easily visible on a sloping hill to the east of the highway. Built in 1853,

The Johnston House

The old depot of the extinct Half Moon Bay Ocean Shore Railroad now serves as a private residence.

this was not only the first Yankee-style farmhouse near Half Moon Bay, but also one of the oldest in the Bay Area.

Johnston, born in Scotland but reared in Pennsylvania and Ohio, joined the California Gold Rush in 1849. With money earned from real estate and part ownership in a San Francisco saloon, the El Dorado, Johnston bought 1162 acres here from the Miramontes and mortgaged this land to buy almost 500 acres more. He dispatched his brother, Thomas, back to Ohio to purchase 800 head of dairy cattle. The livestock was driven across desert and wilderness to Johnston's new ranch land, where most of the newborn calves were lost to grizzly bears.

Starting in 1853, Johnston erected his once elegant home for his Spanish bride, Petra de Jara. There was no loading dock

in the early 1850s, so much of the redwood lumber brought in by ship was dumped overboard into the ocean on an incoming tide and picked up along the beaches as it washed ashore. The house, painted a dazzling white and richly furnished, was a center for much of the refined social life in the area. A descendant of Thomas Johnston tells of how the ship carrying his grandmother, on her way to California to work as a governess, rounded the horn and came up the coast. The ship had remained out of sight of land because of heavy fog, but when the fog lifted her first sight of California was that house high on the hill in a field of golden grain. She knew then that she must visit the house as soon as she could. The result? She met and later married Thomas, James Johnston's brother.

But James Johnston's life and eventually his white house gradually became gray. His Petra died in 1861. In 1878 the bank foreclosed, leaving him only the house and fifteen acres. Johnston died soon afterward. The gradually disintegrating house survived sharecroppers, the 1906 quake, squatters, harsh weather, vandals, and even cattle living in the lower level at one time. Finally, in 1972, a group of concerned citizens formed a foundation to save this important site. By November 1976, they had raised enough money to elevate the house and pour a new foundation. Against the advice of nearby old-timers, one side of the house was removed. Then it happened.

One Saturday, those driving along Highway 1 could glance over at the three windowless sides of the house standing in a

Historic Johnston House, dating back to 1853, was one of the most challenging restorations along the coast.

each timber and beam, and only adding new material when it was really needed. For added strength, the house was sheathed in plywood. A redwood shingle roof was added and the building was again painted white. The Johnston House Foundation rounded up an old door from Pescadero and old window glass from the East Coast. Inside, the kitchen will be restored as a museum. With the help of donations (Box 789, Half Moon Bay, CA 94019), further grants, and the proceeds from the Saturday Thrift Shop (on Purisima where it joins Main Street), the group hopes to furnish the entire interior as it was during the gracious period of the 1860s. Other plans include adding a restroom and importing an old barn to house a senior citizen's center.

Soon after James built his house, his brother, William Johnston, built another house across the road, using wooden pegs instead of nails. William's house, presently in private hands and housing migrant farmworkers, has survived in good shape. Even the shutters are the original ones.

Continuing south on Highway 1, the Redondo Beach Road wends its washboard way to a bluff with a steep path down to the ocean.

Redondo Beach

Next are the green, landscaped *Half Moon Bay Golf Links* (415/726-4438), with their Ocean Colony Estates, homes definitely in the higher income brackets. The 72-par, 18-hole golf course, which overhangs the Pacific, is supposedly the third toughest in Northern California, after Monterey Peninsula's Pebble Beach

Half Moon Bay Golf Links

field of broccoli. Driving back on Sunday, they could see nothing. Strong winds had come up and, as predicted, the partially dismantled house had been blown down.

restoring the Johnston House

However, with the help of grants, George Watson, a consultant to the Smithsonian Institiute, supervised the dissembling of the house and labeled each piece. Luckily, 98 percent of the materials had survived the storm. Other restoration experts began to reassemble the house as if it were a jigsaw puzzle, using the original mortise and tenon construction, refitting and San Francisco's Olympic Club. The P.G.A. pro, incidentally, is Moon Mullins. Contoured greens are kept green with water from the course's own wells plus recycled water. Every golf course has its particular hazards. Here, besides often stiff ocean breezes, fat iridescent ducks sit on the fairways. The small Enterprise Saloon and Restaurant is crowded with golfers and residents at breakfast and lunch. Residents and guests can also use the recently added swim and tennis complex. The pool here can be opened to the air or closed with sliding roof and wall panels.

Miramontes Point South of the golf course, the bumpy *Miramontes Point Road* leads to another high bluff and beach past the Canada Cove Mobile Home Park (adults only). Why is there only one home between the road and golf course? It is full of paper streets and 25-foot-wide lots, the residue of the period when the long defunct Ocean Shore Railroad expected the area to boom. It didn't. The optimistic people who bought lots here decades ago have mostly sold out to the state, but no one is sure what will happen to this relatively untouched area.

Returning to the highway, watch for hawks who find it profitable to sit on the telephone wires overlooking the fields here, a reminder that this area—so close to crowded cities—still retains some of its natural wildness.

where to stay After years of dearth, the *Half Moon Bay Motor Lodge* (Best Western) opened at the southern boundary of Half Moon Bay off Highway 1. Most rooms and suites have balconies and overlook the golf links and ocean. Reserve for weekends (415/726-6301).

The San Benito House (already mentioned), on Main Street and Mill in Half Moon Bay, has eight rooms with bath and two that share a bath. Reserve for weekends (415/726-3425).

RVs are welcome at the *Pelican Point RV Park* (415/726-9100), on Miramontes Road just south of the golf course. The proprietors are friendly and knowledgeable about the area, and there's a small store, laundry room, and club room.

If there's room, self-contained RVs can park for $5.00 a night at Francis State Park Beach, at the end of Kelly Avenue in Half Moon Bay. Turn towards the ocean at the light.

where to eat At the *San Benito House*, Carol Regan is usually in the kitchen every Wednesday through Sunday preparing her "country inn" lunches, dinners, and Sunday brunches. "Her menus are never the same," one diner commented. Dinner consists of three courses with two choices of entree. When possible entrees are local: salmon mousse, perhaps, with artichoke soup and fresh pea salad, along with extra desserts and pastries. Before reserving (wise on weekends), call 415/726-3425 for a recording of what's for dinner.

The small *Garden Deli* adjoining the San Benito House serves soup, salad, and sandwiches, which you can eat in the garden shared with the restaurant.

If you like Mexican food and aren't in a hurry, walk through a pool hall in the small enclosed dining room for dinner at

Santana's, 400 Main. It just might be delicious.

Original Johnny's, breakfast through dinner, and *Ricci's*, breakfast through lunch, are both on Main Street. They attract mostly locals who come for the conversation as much as for the food. Ricci is fast with the pun, serving, for instance, a Papal breakfast (with Polish sausage).

The Happy Cooker in the Strawflower Shopping Center has an advertised modestly priced meal that appeals to the budget-minded and attracts many locals.

The *Cypress House*, at the junction of busy highways 1 and 92, is geared more for tourist wallets, as is the *Shoreline Station*, in the big gray Shoreline Shopping Center off Highway 1 near Kelly.

In the mood for espresso? Try the *Cafe Atelier*, at 510 Kelly Avenue, next to the Alves House. The cafe also serves soups, salads, and pastries.

If the weather is tolerable during the day, you'll probably want to enjoy a picnic lunch at a nearby beach. Fortunately, many establishments already mentioned cater to gourmet picnickers. Try *Cunha's Country Grocery*, the *Half Moon Bay Bakery*, on Main, and *Blanda's*, near Thrifty's in the big shopping center where Highway 92 meets 1.

5

To San Gregorio, Pescadero, La Honda, and the Inland Parks

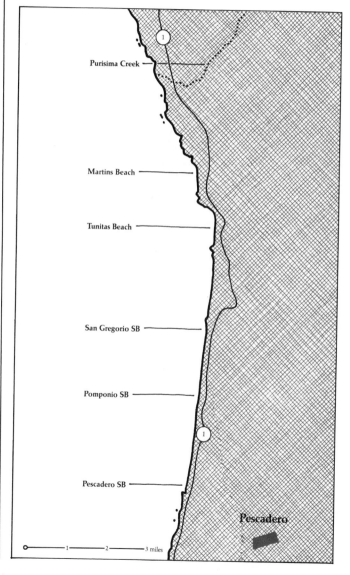

Purisima Creek

Martins Beach

Tunitas Beach

San Gregorio SB

Pomponio SB

Pescadero SB

Pescadero

0 — 1 — 2 — 3 miles

Gas up if necessary before leaving Half Moon Bay, driving south. There are no services directly on Highway 1 for twenty-five miles, although you can get gas until 6 P.M. in San Gregorio. If hunger pangs strike in this isolated area, try to hold out until you reach Santa Cruz, where you'll have a choice of restaurants.

California Scenic Route

Just off the highway soon after you pass the Canada Cove Mobile Home settlement is a sign: *Scenic Route,* showing a golden poppy waving against a snow-capped mountain under a blue sky. An official scenic route is a roadway whose surroundings are so unique, beautiful, or historic that it has been put under state protection. But first an advisory committee, highway officials, and legislators have to agree that the area is worth saving. When the Director of Transportation is satisfied that local authorities will pass enough zoning regulations to protect the surroundings from billboards, junkyards, and similar blights, these special markers are put up. Only a fraction of California's roads wear these golden poppy signs, but at least a few miles of *this* scenic coastline are now officially protected.

an ostrich hill

Nearby, to your right, if you think you see two ostriches standing next to a vaguely Victorian house on a hill, you're not hallucinating. These ungainly birds are pets, and you occasionally see advertisements in the Half Moon Bay Review for sterile ostrich eggs on sale.

Purisima ghost town

The *Higgins-Purisima Road* returns to Highway 1 at the ghost town of *Purisima,* where you'll see a small, white Victorian farmhouse with fish-scale shingling and an original water wheel. About the only reminder of the past population remaining since the schoolhouse burned is the old cemetery, overgrown with weeds and poison oak, on a knoll on the southeast side of the intersection.

There's a small waterfall at the south end of *Purisima Creek,* but you may not feel it's worth paying admission to the now-private area and the struggle in to see it.

The *Lobitos Creek* cutoff is the next road to the left, about a mile further south. The cutoff and the *Lobitos Creek Road,* just inland, connect with the beautiful, narrow *Tunitas Creek Road,* flanked by redwoods and hideaway cabins, which finally twists its way up to Skyline Boulevard.

The many tall poles on the seaward side of the Lobitos Creek Road still serve the *Marine Bureau and Radio Station of I.T.T. World Communications, Inc.,* and the small building is jammed with equipment for communicating with ships at sea by Morse code, a dying art, according to employees. The men report proudly that even now, on occasion, they intercept messages of distress from small freighters or ships without fancy communication equipment, perhaps on the other side of the world, and relay the S.O.S. signal on to the nearest rescue operation.

*White-painted barn and fences set against a eucalyptus grove
make this ranch at Lobitos Creek a photographer's favorite.*

Probably the most photographed farm along the coastside, especially during pumpkin season, is nestled in the Lobitos Creek Valley on the landward side, just south. In October, cars are often stopped just off the highway while their drivers snap color pictures of the white farm buildings and grazing animals against the deep-green hillsides and the rows of orange pumpkins on the black earth.

The road here loops back and connects with Verde Road. All these backroads are pleasant for biking as well as driving.

In the slower paced days of horse travel, the town of Lobitos and many other areas next to creeks along the coastside were the sites of anticipated villages. In 1892, Lobitos was called "headquarters for oil wells," representing the acme of optimism. At least here several buildings are standing, including one large, beautifully renovated house that doubled as the Garret Art Gallery for several years.

Many coastside maps, even an old one put out by the Half Moon Bay Chamber of Commerce, show towns—complete with streets and boulevards—that never existed. Promoters, busy selling lots around the turn of the century, were responsible for most of these "paper" towns. Subsequent zoning regulations have made it impossible for most owners to build on these near-the-ocean lots.

Martin's Beach

Martin's Beach, next south on Highway 1, charges a toll and closes at sunset. It's a handkerchief-sized beach chock full of cars, picnickers, transistors, and fishermen. A small store peddles such beach equipment as beer, suntan lotion, and hotdogs. The steep dirt slope to the beach is peppered with small cottages owned by the residents, although they do not own the land.

You might bring along a two-man jump net and try surf netting for smelt here during the spring or summer. Smelt come into the turbulent breaker area to spawn. They release eggs that adhere to sand particles even through heavy surf action until they hatch in ten to twelve days. It's a memorable sight to witness the smelt crowding in. Early Indians believed that the tiny fish came in to dance on their tails by the full moon.

Tunitas Beach and Gordon's Chute

Next south *Tunitas Beach* (straddling Tunitas Creek), was once a transfer point for the defunct Ocean Shore Railroad. It was also here that Alexander Gordon—trying to make a port where none existed—built *Gordon's Chute*, at a 45-degree angle from the 100-foot bluff to rocks constantly battered by waves. The chute was designed to shunt produce from land to ships waiting below, though ship captains hated to anchor in the roiling surf. Besides, the friction of the long slide usually burned holes in the produce bags or they burst open when they hit the deck. In 1885 a storm demolished the bankrupt enterprise. Now only the eye bolts are visible on the few occasions when the rocks are uncovered at low tide.

There's a legend that a sea monster resides in a cave in the turbulent area between these rocks and Martin's Beach, sometimes sticking his head up "high as the mast of a fishing boat." According to most descriptions, this beast resembles the Loch Ness Monster: a monster head—whatever that is—followed by a series of black oily humps. Early sailors often saw monsters at sea. What present-day monster hunters might see is a school of seals or sea lions, or possibly a line of porpoises playing follow-the-leader, dipping and diving in turbulent water.

When they were young, the pioneer artist Galen Wolf and his brother attempted to visit the sea monster's cave. But they decided that monster hunting was too dangerous when a gray, curling monster of a wave, which could have been fatal, chased them over the flat rocky tables and at least twenty feet up the steep cliff.

Note and warning: Tunitas is a private beach with fences, locked gates, and no-trespassing warnings. To get to the ocean, pay the modest fee at Martin's Beach to the north, or at Nude Beach directly south, or wait for San Gregorio State Beach, about a mile and a half farther south.

Nude Beach

Nude (or Bare-Bottom) Beach, next south, charges a small admission fee. This beach, two miles long, seems to attract mainly males, although females are admitted. It's "free" in the sense that no holds are barred, and dozens of small planes buzz the beach on weekends to take in the sights. At very low tides curiosity seekers wade around the rocks at the south end of this beach. One road leads in to Nude Beach between two decayed barns, a mile

San Gregorio State Beach offers a broad, wind-protected strand and a freshwater lagoon at the mouth of San Gregorio Creek.

south of Tunitas bridge, and another access road is just north of San Gregorio Beach.

The official non-nude *San Gregorio State Beach* (8.5 miles south of Half Moon Bay) is usually packed on sunny weekends. The charge for using the beach is $2.00 per car. A truck is often on hand to sell coffee, sandwiches, and snacks. There are restrooms. There's a lagoon that's warm (well, not freezing), and high bluffs partially protect the beach from winds. Still in the planning stage are extensive camping and picnic areas on the landward side of Highway 1.

Right outside the park, across from the turnoff to San Gregorio, is a state

San Gregorio State Beach

marker in honor of the *Portola Expedition*, which camped nearby on its bedraggled march north in 1769.

San Gregorio

San Gregorio (population approximately 150), is about a mile inland (the turnoff is directly across from the beach). This community was a popular resort at the turn of the century before the redwoods were logged out, but now, like other small towns in the vicinity, it has shrunk. Note the little nostalgia-evoking one-room schoolhouse, now empty, on your right. Although it has no running water and only primitive sanitation, when the school district put the building up for auction several years ago, more than sixty interested people attended the event. But the owners of the surrounding acres—part of the original Rancho San Gregorio—were determined to regain possession and did. The town itself, surrounded by green rolling hills, looks as if it were straight out of New England.

Peterson & Alsford General Store

Don't miss the action, daily from nine to six, at the *Peterson & Alsford General Store.* Tennessee Ernie Ford is supposed to bring cronies by to see what a country store should look like. You'll find almost everything you need here and more: saddles, saws, salami, clothing, wine, hardware, pot-bellied stoves, licorice sticks, bean pots, and—you name it. A tiny post office adjoins. Sit at the eight-stool bar here and exchange gossip with the local artichoke and sheep farmers.

For many decades the main attraction at the store was Eric Alsford, the spirited pioneer who ran it along with his nephew and other family members. After Eric died,

The busy general store at San Gregorio is an example of California's Mission Revival architecture, altered by gas pumps and a phone booth.

in his late eighties, the store was sold to five young professional people from Palo Alto, including a lawyer and a professor. "We're making enough to exist on," one of the owners reported, "and it is a good life. I think the best thing is the air—so fresh— and we hear coyotes at night."

These days the store's clientele consists of a younger bearded crowd who indulge in much shaking of dice. Cowboy boots are for sale on top of the wine counter next to the gourmet cheeses, and now there's a piano. You can buy t-shirts and beaked caps with the Peterson & Alsford motif. At first glance the store looks the same as it has for years, but there's something missing—Eric.

San Gregorio House

Cross the highway south on the Stage Road, and behind the service station you'll see a well-preserved old hotel, complete with full-length balcony and the inevitable wooden water tank nearby. Originally called the *San Gregorio House*, it was built in the 1850s and was a "popular resort," where people with nationally famous names sometimes stopped for hunting and fishing. Now the building is a private residence, and on sunny days old men sit outside on benches and reminisce about the early days. A primitive bar, which sells only beer and peanuts, is open sporadically in a weathered building behind a rusty gas pump.

In the late 1800s, San Gregorio boasted a branch of the firm of *Levy Brothers*, a dry goods and general merchandise store. The Levy's also acquired ownership of the stagecoach line from San Mateo plus the *Wells Fargo Express* agency.

stage road to Pescadero

If you continue south on Stage Road you'll eventually arrive at *Pescadero* after a long, lonely trek. Some automobile tourists (and bicyclists)—though not all—are enthusiastic about the rolling golden hills and quiet farms on this route.

La Honda

At the apex of a triangle with San Gregorio and Pescadero at its western edge is *La Honda* (population 525). It's an easy nine miles inland on the San Gregorio turnoff from Highway 1, or what seems forever, when driving on Skyline Boulevard. Early pioneer Nellie Hedgpeth reported from La Honda several decades ago: "The second story of the hotel was full of guests, and the woods around were filled with campers . . . very festive, with strings of Japanese lanterns and flags." One camp was called Up-Enough because of the steep climb the horses had to face.

the bandit-built store

The *Pioneer Market* in La Honda sometimes likes to think of itself as the next-door successor to the "Bandit-Built Store," which burned to the ground in 1959. In 1877, John H. Sears (who settled in this area in 1861–62) started to erect a new store in the middle of La Honda over a thirty-foot-deep bear pit. Legend had it that the Younger Brothers, who later hooked up with the Jesse James gang, helped build it. "Not so," say some reputable historians. "How could they help in 1877 when they pulled their last big robbery in 1876 and were promptly put in the pen for many years?"

The hotel is no longer, nor is the old store. Many towering redwoods are still left, however, to lure tourists. La Honda gained notoriety when author Ken Kesey moved into the area with his family, friends, and psychedelic van. But the pressure was put on, and Kesey and friends departed.

local bars

In addition to gazing at the big trees and enjoying the usual sunshine (some-

Boots and Saddle Restaurant at La Honda lifts a neon toast to the towering redwoods around its parking lot.

times too much), you might canvas the town's three bars. *Boots and Saddle,* on the south edge of town, is a neighborhood bar with pickup trucks parked outside and a cowboy accent. At the *La Honda Lodge* the cowboys use more four-letter words. *Apple-Jack's* is delightfully old and seedy and a pleasant place to drink your beer.

The string of arts and crafts shops that used to adjoin the post office in a wooden line are no more. All through the coastside colorful little shops peddling candles and handicrafts spread their wings briefly, like moths, and then die. Baw's restaurant-bakery has been replaced by *Roger's Back Yard,* a restaurant sporting the sign "No shirt, no shoes, no service." The diners who enjoy the homemade soups and entrees here definitely wear shoes. La Honda, like the towns all along this mountain redwood area, attracts a smorgasbord of types: cowboys—fact or fantasy—riding pickup trucks, young people with bare feet and long hair, and people attending religious retreats or schools. (There's a religious institution across from the La Honda Shopping Center.)

About the only annual event worth a look in La Honda if you happen to be in the area occurs in the middle of July. Then flags blossom along the highway to announce La Honda Days' Celebration, with barbecue and festivities. It's put on by the La Honda Fire Brigade.

the Big Inland Parks

Most tourists who drive along the La Honda Road (Highway 84) have not come to sample the pleasures of La Honda (although there is a campground and a small motel here). They are on their way to one of the big parks within easy driving distance.

Sam McDonald County Park

The 850 acres of steep *Sam McDonald County Park,* three miles west of La Honda on Pescadero Road, are to be enjoyed on foot. The northwesterly 400 acres are mainly covered with lush redwoods. The other 450-acre portion is mostly open ridge; you can see the sweep of the Pacific Ocean as you hike along the four-mile Ridge Trail. The Towne Trail leads from park headquarters to the new *Pescadero Creek Park*—5700 acres of redwood forests strictly for daytime hiking between 8 A.M. and 5 P.M. One and a half miles along the Towne Trail is a Danish designed wood hiker's hut erected by the Sierra Club. You can reserve overnight bunk space here by calling 415/327-8111 on weekday afternoons.

Most of the park's campgrounds are for organized groups who want to get away from a parking lot full of cars, with preference given to San Mateo County groups. Originally the park was geared for younger groups, such as Boy and Girl Scouts, but park officials discovered that many adult groups prefer this type of camping. Get specific information on camping reservations from the Park Supervisor (415/727-0403). For information on any San Mateo County park call Parks and Recreation, County Government Center, Redwood City, CA 94063 (415/364-5600, extension 2393).

reserving campsites at county parks

If you just want to picnic, you'll find a few facilities near the park headquarters. Before you leave, be sure to visit the *Heritage Grove,* twenty-seven acres of magnificent old-growth redwoods, which adjoins the park to the northwest. The grove is on Alpine Road, one mile west of Pescadero Road.

Heritage Grove

San Mateo County Memorial Park is probably the most beautiful of the inland coastside parks. Drive south a half-mile from La Honda, where signs clearly direct you left on Alpine Road, then right on the Pescadero Road for about six miles.

San Mateo County Memorial Park

Memorial Park has 133 overnight campsites among sun-dappled redwoods; additional campsites can be opened for crowded weekends. A large, dammed-up swimming spot has a sunny strip of sand nearby for sunbasking, the creek is stocked with rainbow trout during tourist season, and the park contains many miles of lovely hiking trails. There's a full schedule of nature films, walks, and campfire programs, and an unofficial program of watching bluejays steal food during the day and raccoons thieve at night. Fees here are moderate for daytime use; the overnight fee is $5.00 per car.

Portola State Park, at the bottom of a twisting narrow road, is almost ten miles from La Honda and a good 21.5 miles inland from Pescadero. You can also reach this park by driving west from Redwood City on Highway 84, south on Highway 35 (Skyline Boulevard) for seven miles, and then west on Alpine Road.

Portola State Park

Portola Park has fifty-two overnight campsites, plus three group-camping areas that can be reserved. During the summer tourist season, the creek is stocked weekly with rainbow trout. The State Fish and Game personnel try to vary planting times and to keep their efforts secret.

Fees are $2.00 for day use, $5.00 a car overnight. As with the other parks on the coastside, reservations are recommended during the summer or for long weekends.

Get information on reservations (and on the entire California state park system) from the Department of Parks and Recreation, P.O. Box 2390, Sacramento, CA

reserving at state parks

95811; Ticketron offices in Sears stores; or call Ticketron (800/622-0904) for the closest outlet.

Portola State Park's many miles of hiking trails include a self-guided Sequoia nature trail that leads you past an old redwood whose heartwood has been burned out after many fires but whose top is still green.

Castle Rock State Park

Nearby as the crow flies, but actually off Skyline (Highway 35) is *Castle Rock State Park*, geared mainly for hikers. There's group camping by reservation here, several camp sites for families, a hiker's shelter, and an observation platform overlooking Castle Rock Falls.

Butano State Park

Probably the least visited of the inland parks in this area is *Butano State Park*. It's near the coast, five miles south of Pescadero and three miles east of Highway 1 on Cloverdale Road. There are forty-six overnight campsites in this 2200-acre redwood park, and since it's a Bikecentennial camp, bikers and hikers can camp overnight for 50¢. Because you have to park and walk in to many campsites, the park is exceptionally quiet. This makes it ideal for campers who want to get away from it all. Indians first picked the area as ideally beautiful for gatherings. As for hiking trails, there are fifteen lovely miles. One trail leads to an overlook with a panoramic view of the ocean and Año Nuevo Island. You'll have this view, that is, if there's no fog billowing along the shore. However, nothing is perfect, and Butano Park is inclined to be dusty.

The biggest park, over thirteen thousand acres, is *Big Basin Redwoods State Park*, in the Santa Cruz Mountains. See page 106 for information.

Big Basin

Besides the huge redwoods and Douglas firs, at all these parks, especially near streams, you'll probably see such typical plants as western azalea, California blackberry, and the infamous poison oak, with its three shiny leaves and the ability to present anyone who touches it with days of agonizing itching.

typical flora and fauna

You're also sure to see at least some of the following coastside animals. The *brush rabbit*, small and brown, with short ears, usually hops about in thick underbrush at twilight. The *raccoon*, a gray bandit with a black mask, often explores garbage cans at night. A *striped* or *spotted skunk* is better seen, not smelled. *Gray foxes*, with white under their necks and black tips on their bushy tails, are quite common. *Merriam chipmunks*, with rusty-colored sides and white bellies, will probably accost you in a park. When they scold, their tails jerk. You're also sure to see a *western gray squirrel*, gray with a white belly and a large bushy tail, scuttling among the large trees. *Harvest* and *deer mice* are very common (ask anyone with a cabin in the area), as are *wood rats*. You can often spot the huge wood rat nests of twigs in the branches of trees or shrubs. You can sometimes see *black-tailed deer*, and *pocket gophers* advertise their presence by mounds of dirt on the ground. The *Virginia opossum* is gray, with a white face and a naked scaly tail. A *bobcat*—if it's really a bobcat and not a domestic cat gone wild—has a reddish body, a white belly, and a small bobbed tail. At dusk you often see the *California myotis bat,* a mouse-size mammal, catching insects.

Pomponio State Beach

Meanwhile, back along the ocean shore, *Pomponio State Beach,* 1.5 miles south of San Gregorio, charges $2.00 a car for day use. This fee gives you access to 410 acres of beautiful and protected recreational area, paved parking for eighty cars, picnic facilities, and restrooms (but no drinking water). Some artists consider Pomponio, with its marshy lagoon and high bluff, the most photogenic beach along this stretch. It was named for a renegade Indian who terrorized the coastside during the mission days. According to some historians, Pomponio felt justified in his activities. After he escaped from a mission, which he felt had kept him and other Indians in virtual slavery, being a bandit was the only occupation open to him.

Back in Pomponio Canyon some wildlife still prowls at night. As late as 1980 ranchers and others reported seeing coyotes, bobcats, and foxes, and—whether real or imaginary—there are still occasional rumors of a mountain lion farther back in the hills.

Pescadero State Beach

There's no charge for using *Pescadero State Beach,* about three miles farther south. The beach is long, lovely, and popular, with enough variation to please everyone, but you can usually find a secluded nook, and there are a few primitive restrooms. To the north, you can slide down sand dunes and there's a creek big enough for children to play in. A favorite sport is to float down to the mouth of the creek on rubber rafts. Steelhead runs occur each year here where the creek meets the ocean.

poke poling for eels

To the south is a rocky area with excellent tidepools. Where there are rocks there's not only *rock-fishing* but also *poke poling* for monkey-face eels with bamboo poles 12 to 15 feet long. The intrepid poke poler wades out at a very low tide and pokes the pole—baited with mussel, cutfish, or shrimp—into crevasses or between rocks. Since the eel retreats rapidly and wraps itself around anything available, you need strength as well as patience to pull one out if it takes the bait.

Pescadero Marsh

Inland, across the highway along the road to Pescadero is the 555-acre *Pescadero Marsh Natural Preserve.* Stay on the trails and enjoy the quiet panorama of nature without, however, dogs or horses—they are banned. Besides the distant, wide-angle view of Pescadero, you might glimpse deer, raccoons, foxes, skunks, and rare birds such as the kite.

Farther back, great blue herons nest in eucalyptus trees and stalk fish in the shallow waters of the swampy area. Among frequent visitors, besides the great blue herons, are the crested white herons (also as tall as 6 feet) and the shorter egrets and ibis. This group seems to favor standing on one leg. You'll probably see the pair of resident marsh hawks circling above, reddish-backed cinnamon teal cutting through the water and perhaps bitterns fluffing out their feathers. Add to this a background of music, as the yellow throat, the Bay Area's only resident warbler, pours out its song.

Mallard and pintail ducks visit here also, and red-winged blackbirds are usually around, along with so many other species that the National Audubon Society helped add 340 acres to the original 215-acre preserve. For information on occasional birding excursions write the Audubon Society, 1009 Laguna Avenue, Burlingame, CA 94010. If you're taking pictures of birds you'll need a telephoto lens and high-speed film so you can snap the photo at your camera's fastest shutter speed. Otherwise you'll merely get a faraway dot or a blur.

shore birds

Back across the road at Pescadero State Beach, you may glimpse some of these shore birds along the ocean. *Sandpipers* are tiny shorebirds that run back and forth with great self-importance, constantly probing for food and twittering. When they're running along the shore they sometimes look as if they were on wheels. You'll see them all year except summer, when they're off in their Arctic breeding grounds. *Sanderlings* are the most abundant sandpipers. They feed at the very edge of the surf, barely rushing back in time. When startled, they emit a short, sharp "twit." Other sandpipers are hard to identify. Many birdwatchers call them all "peeps."

Dowitchers are stolid-looking birds with long straight bills. They eat with a sewing-machine motion.

Killdeers are robin-size, with a white band on the forehead and two black convict bands across a white chest. Their cry is more nearly "ki-dee." They're great actors.

If you get close to a killdeer's eggs (in a shallow scoop—no nest) it will hop ahead of you, dragging a wing pitifully as if it were broken. When it decides it's lured you away far enough, the bird bolts for home.

Plovers are the size of a killdeer but have a different coloration.

Curlews are large, brown birds with long bills that curve downward. *Godwits* are a mottled brown; their bills curve upward. *Willets* are smaller cronies of godwits and curlews, and much more numerous. Identify them in flight by the dramatic white stripes on their black wings. They emit a shrill "whee-wee-wee." *Avocets* have blue bills that turn upward, white undersides, and wide black stripes on back and side to the tail.

common sea birds

The most common sea birds are gulls, the noisy, scolding scavengers that help keep beaches clean. *Western gulls* are the most noticeable. They are large and dark; look for the heavy yellow beak. *Heermann's gulls* have white heads that contrast with their gray bodies and scarlet bills. They're the gulls that emit that mad laughing. They sometimes follow a pelican's thrilling dive to snatch his catch. *California gulls* are white; you'll see them here only in winter, for they nest inland. These gulls were credited with saving the crops of Utah pioneers from plagues of grasshoppers.

Cormorants look grotesque as they perch on offshore rocks, with their long, snaky necks and long, slightly hooked beaks. These large black birds are superb at fishing. Some Japanese use them as slave fishers, placing a ring around the neck of each bird so it can't swallow any large fish it catches.

Brown pelicans look even more bizarre than cormorants. Their big, pouched bills are so awkward they seem to rest them on their breasts for support. However, if you've seen one plummet after fish like a dive bomber, you'll never forget the sight. For many years, because of the high percentage of DDT in the fish they ate, brown pelicans' eggs were so thin-shelled that scarcely any hatched. When DDT was banned, the birds recovered, and you now see streamers of them along the coast.

Grebes, or *hell-divers*, hang out on the surf line or in lagoons. They are superb divers. *California murres* fly in lines close to the water with rapid wingstrokes. *Scoters* are diving ducks, often seen this side of the breakers. *Coots* (mud hens) are numerous in freshwater ponds. On shore, they waddle awkwardly, like old men.

inland birds

To complete this brief look at birds, go inland just a short distance, get your binoculars ready, and you might see some of these.

Steller's jays start scolding the minute you step into their conifer-forest headquarters. They're dark blue, with a large near-black crest, and are impudent thieves.

Allen's hummingbirds flit and hover wherever there are bright flowers. They have green backs and brilliant throats, sides, and tails.

California quail are those gray-and-brown birds with black-and-white faces, plus black, curving head plumes, that scuttle across your road or path into bushes.

Their cry sounds like "Chicago."

Goldfinches look like canaries, but they're not.

If you see tiny brown birds with black and white streaks, they probably belong to one of the many species of *sparrows.*

The female *house finch* looks like other sparrows, but the male boasts a bright crimson head and breast. You'll probably see house finches lined up on a telephone wire.

Note: if you want to learn more about coastline birds, see the *Field Guide to Western Birds* by Roger Tory Peterson (published by Houghton-Mifflin) or *Birds of North America* by Chandler S. Robbins, Bertel Bruun, Herbert S. Zim, and Arthur Singer (published by Golden Press).

beachcombing tips

Not everyone has the patience for birdwatching, but almost everyone likes *beachcombing*, so here are a few words on where to find seashore treasures and what to do with them.

Driftwood hunting is best in areas where a creek or stream empties into the ocean. Pescadero Beach is one place that fills the bill. The best time to hunt is after a winter storm; by the end of summer pickings are usually slim. However, at any time of the year occasional freak summer winds and currents bring in driftwood, bottles, and fishing floats covered with gooseneck barnacles. These repulsive-looking animals dry up when left in the sun; scrape them off your booty and you may uncover a stunning piece.

The tools you need for driftwood collecting are a creative eye, a rope to drag the big pieces, and a knapsack to carry the smaller ones. You might also carry a shovel and a husky knife or small saw, to help liberate the bigger pieces.

To clean driftwood, remove fragments of bark with a screwdriver or a knife with a dull end. Use a sharp knife or an icepick to pry out knots or embedded rocks (although often these are an asset). At home you may cut off frayed ends; then use a file or rasp to make the cuts look weathered.

Clean off your prize with a brush soft enough to leave no marks, unless you want a grained effect. If the piece isn't weathered or light enough to suit you, you might leave it in the sun and water it daily for a few weeks. A quicker way is to use a commercial wood bleach and brush on neutralizer when the wood reaches the shade you want. You can finish the piece with a clear wood preservative or varnish sealer. Or you can paint on a thin coat of shingle or siding stain. Some purists insist on merely rubbing in clear furniture wax with a clean shoebrush.

The Office of Marine Zoology of the U.S. Geological Survey pays a 50¢ reward if you report finding one of their yellow plastic drifters, which they drop into the ocean at specific locations in order to study the currents. When the drifters sink, they are carried along by currents in the near-bottom water. Information on where to report your find is on the yellow disk.

As noted earlier, if you pick up *sand dollars*, those beautiful but fragile shells showing the imprint of a star, you can break one carefully and look at those little white particles in the center. Whether you decide they look like angels or doves, their purpose is less poetic; they constitute the sand dollar's alimentary system. Zoologists call them Aristotle's lanterns.

Be on the lookout for colorful glass fishing floats that have escaped from their job of holding up fishing nets. Best float hunting is on wide, sandy beaches after a vigorous early spring storm. On that lucky day or night when the floats wash in, pounce immediately. They're usually picked up in hours, although patient beachcombers who look in piles of driftwood or seaweed may be rewarded up to several days later. However, since the advent of plastic, about the only place you'll find glass floats soon will be in a souvenir shop.

Bottles, etched and frosted by sand and sea, may not be valuable to knowledgeable collectors, but they are still considered finds. If the bottle already is or is turning an iridescent purple, it is old. Other things that may prove its age: mold marks that don't come to the top, indicating that the lip was added later; on spirits bottles, a lack of the embossed warning, "Federal Law Forbids Resale"; and pontil marks—they're the roundish marks left by the iron or steel rod used for fashioning hot glass—on the bottom of the bottle.

Warning: the hobby of bottle-collecting can become addictive. Some avid collectors pore over old maps and pick the brains of oldtimers to discover dumps or sawmill sites where odds are good they'll find valuable bottles under debris or brush. The San Mateo and Santa Cruz mountains are full of old lumbering sites. Some dedicated bottle buffs even dig at the sites of old privies, on the theory that someone's great-grandfather may have tossed an empty whiskey bottle in the privy rather than have great-grandmother catch him with the forbidden evidence.

Pescadero The town—or perhaps village is the right word— of *Pescadero*, two miles from the turnoff at Highway 1, is just far enough inland to be at the edge of the sun belt. Optimists say its population is 1000. Others contend, approvingly, that it has shrunk from 700 to 500. And a spritely 88-year-old inhabitant doesn't believe it holds more than 300. Whatever the official count, Pescadero is definitely "country," containing nostalgic reminders of the way we used to live. It's not just the cowboy hats that many inhabitants affect; it's the leisurely old-country lifestyle. At one home, for instance, you're likely to find a hand-penned sign on the front door reading, "Back at three. The coffee is perking in the kitchen. Come on in and pour yourself a cup."

Originally the town was mainly Portuguese, but many of the old frame houses—even those dolled up with Victorian facades—seem to be straight from New England. Legend has it that when the *S.S. Columbia* was wrecked near Pigeon Point in 1896, most of her cargo of white paint was liberated by the inhabitants, who used it lavishly to paint their houses, with their descendants keeping up the white-paint tradition to this day. Why was the town named Pescadero, meaning fishing place? Perhaps it was for the speckled

A eucalyptus-shaded knoll in the local cemetery overlooks the small white-painted hamlet of Pescadero.

trout that once inhabited the creek.

The main "fishing" done in early days was by men who rowed out in small wooden boats to harpoon the giant gray whales and tow them ashore for rendering. There are still a few old trying pots around Pescadero and recipes incorporating whale oil have been passed from generation to generation.

Pescadero boasts several more modern amenities; there's even a clothing store. More interesting to tourists, however, is the *Williamson General Store*, which probably carries everything you'll need. It's also a gathering spot for many old-timers. You can find out a lot about the area from Harriet Dias, who helps to run the store. She is also impresario of the parade for the quaint *Festival of the Holy Ghost, the Chamarita,* which takes place on the sixth Sunday after Easter. (See page 57 for the origins of this folk festival.) The parade marches to the Catholic Church at 10 A.M., then retraces its steps to the main highway after noon. High-school bands, former queens, horsemen, wandering minstrels, the newly crowned queen, and future royalty all march proudly by. Afterwards everyone is invited to a free barbecue. The queens are royally treated. One sign along the main street reads, "All queens admitted free."

Festival of the Holy Ghost

Duarte's, right off the Pescadero Highway on Stage Road (Main Street) is another unofficial headquarters for local inhabitants, partly because it's the only restaurant and tavern for miles around. The tavern was started in 1895 when Frank Duarte asked a friend to bring back a barrel of whiskey from Santa Cruz. Frank set the barrel on a plank and was in business. In the mid-thirties, Frank, Jr., and his wife, Emma, started the restaurant, which appealed to the local dairymen and farmers because of the generous portions and modest prices. These days, Frank's grandson, Ron, runs it. Emma, now in her seventies, still retains her strong personality, still

Duarte's

bakes the pies (the olallieberry pie is pure nectar), and can still turn a canned oyster sandwich into a gourmet feast. The restaurant—open seven days a week—is famous for its artichoke omelets and soup. Cioppino feeds are held every other Saturday during crab season, but they're so popular reservations are necessary (415/879-0464).

The Pescadero Store, a minute gem of a shop run by Phylis Gandy and Meredith Reynolds, is tucked into the corner of Duarte's at 200 Stage Road. It's open Tuesday through Sunday from 11 A.M. to 6ish. Gifts include porcelain by Miriam Owens, wildflower honey by a local beekeeper, afghans and crocheted hats by B. Allen, stepping stones by Dan Geraci, bird feeders from La Honda pottery, paintings of coast scenery, redwood burl clocks by Gandy's father, and dozens more hand-picked, hand-crafted items. The inventory is im-

The Pescadero Store

The artichoke, one of the coastside's biggest commerical crops, is the edible blossom of a giant thistle.

pressive for such a tiny store. The larger Pescadero Country Store in back of the Duarte's parking lot sells mainly Western clothing and gear.

The Carrier Pigeon

Just south of the highway on Main Street, is *The Carrier Pigeon*, an antique and what-not emporium, in an old blacksmith shop. Here you can browse through such items as opium scales, quilts, bottles, and old trundle beds plus driftwood and artifacts galore. Unfortunately, the store is rarely open. If you'd like a look, ask around for Mrs. Louise Buell, the owner, and she might open up. The Buells restored the two old balconied houses across the street and are a good source of information about other old houses.

Tony Oliveira, the "antique man"

An even larger antique shop on Pescadero Road a mile east of the turnoff to Highway 1 is run by *Tony Oliveira*, the antique man, who once shined shoes in Santa Cruz to acquire enough money to buy collectibles. Eventually he parlayed his money into a shopping center in Aptos. In 1978 he decided the Santa Cruz area was becoming too crowded, so he bought sixteen acres in Pescadero and remodeled an old barn to house his antiques. He is open every Friday, Saturday, and Sunday from 11 A.M. to 4 P.M. You'll find almost everything collectible inside, including Indian blankets, handicrafts, and baskets; old Depression glass; antique tins and boxes; and a whole barnful more.

Artichoke Festival

Tony's sixteen acres were the site of Pescadero's *First Annual Artichoke Festival*, held on Labor Day, 1980, and sure to be repeated. The occasion was festive, with children, cats, and chickens running

Pescadero's Annual Artichoke Festival which takes place each Labor Day weekend, features a flea market, antiques, and entertainment.

about and long lines of people waiting to sample the French-fried artichokes. Artichoke t-shirts were popular and vendors sold everything from antiques to pots to plants to food to art.

One of the booths, which sold oil paintings on shingles from an 118-year-old barn, was run by the town artist, *Molly Ramolla*. Molly, who was born in Berlin, is versatile and inventive. Besides working in watercolors, egg tempura, and printmaking techniques, she turns out papyruslike "paintings" using the reeds of a nearby bullrush that are similar to Egyp-

Molly Ramolla, the town artist and her gallery

tian reeds. This process involves months of soaking, pounding, and drying the reeds in the sun. The eventual result somewhat resembles a two-dimensional etching in warm earthtones.

Molly has her own art gallery and studio in a rented carriage house at 292 Stage Road in Pescadero. The gallery is open Friday, Saturday, and Sunday from 10 A.M. to 7 P.M. and by appointment (415/879-0706). Molly's husband, the town writer, *Charles Jones*, has a small office in the back. He is best known for a book published by the Sierra Club several years ago, *A Separate Place*, about the nearby San Gregorio/La Honda area, with its mix of nature, man, and animals. Jones, in voluntary exile from the academic world, holds many degrees, including ones in biology, philosophy, and anthropology.

Molly and Charles met in 1975 at San Francisco's funky Eagle Cafe. They married soon afterward and decided to follow the dream of so many writers and artists— to live by their own creativity. So far, they have succeeded. They rent a small white house next door to the gallery, raise chickens, and grow their own vegetables. Charles has lived in the area for over a decade, but he says—with amusement— that he will probably not be fully accepted until he is buried and has spent several decades underground. Yet when he and Molly talk about their adopted home they become evangelistic about belonging, at last, to a community small enough to enable people to know and care for each other, yet within easy driving distance of a large city. Their fellow inhabitants, they point

Charles Jones, the town writer

out, pursue a wonderful combination of occupations and speak an assortment of English, Spanish, Italian, and Portuguese. This diversity, Molly and Charles feel, is a great asset. Because the population is so varied, the community has learned to be tolerant.

It's worth a few minutes to take a look at some of the old buildings and water towers in this quaint town. Straight ahead on Stage Road, Pescadero Street, or Main Street (they're all one and the same) you'll see the big tower and spire of the *Pescadero Community Church*, started in 1867. It's of white wood, but the siding was carefully made to simulate stone. If you're in the area on the first Friday and Saturday of December, you might take in the church bazaar where you'll find handiwork and handicrafts and home-baked bread and other delectables. You can also buy lunch here.

Farther ahead on a lopsided hill is the Pescadero cemetery, with its nostalgic record of the past. One side is called Mount Hope, the other Saint Anthony's. Walk up to the top for a panoramic view of the village and rolling farmlands on its outskirts. The cemetery is at its spectacular best in late summer, when it is covered with hundreds of vivid rosy pink naked ladies (*Amaryllis belladonna*).

Saint Anthony's Catholic Church, built in 1870, is on North Street. As its name implies, North Street is north of the Pescadero Highway. Opposite the church is a typical and well-maintained house of the same period. The log cabin on nearby Goulson Street was not built by some early

Pescadero Community Church

cemeteries

Saint Anthony's Catholic Church

pioneer homes

pioneer, but was erected within the last fifty years as a Boy Scout headquarters.

The *Alexander Moore house*, the first frame house in Pescadero, is no more. Vandals and then a fire destroyed it. The son of the city's founder built the house in 1853 just outside the present city limits on Pescadero Creek Road at the Cloverdale turnoff. He used timbers brought from Santa Cruz by ox cart. The *Weeks home*, also on Pescadero Creek Road, is still standing. When it was built in 1856 it copied the general plan of the Moore house. In fact, most of the town consists of slight variations on the pioneer house style.

Nearby, also on Pescadero Creek Road, are the impressive stone pillars of the Crown Nine Rancho, formerly the Crown Nine Motorcycle Park and soon to be again if plans are approved for thirty miles of riding trails, a fifty-site campground, and a picnic site.

strawflower factory

En route to the Weeks home, on Pescadero Creek Road, you'll see fields of flowers and the *strawflower factory* of John Dias and Sons. Women take the flowers home to wire. The flowers are then dried in ovens for twenty-four hours, sorted into bouquets, and packed. So many visitors asked to be shown around this colorful factory, it interfered with business, so tours are no longer given. However, anyone may look out over the fields of flowers waiting their turn to be dried.

If you're coming from the south, Pescadero, rather than San Gregorio, is the best entry way to most of the big inland parks. Stay on the Pescadero Creek Road for *San McDonald County Park* or *San Mateo County Park*, next door (see pages 74, 75). Your route twists up to Alpine Road, where you can turn right to *Portola State Park* or left to *La Honda;* either direction leads shortly to Skyline Boulevard. It's all fascinating country, with big trees and occasional overlook vistas.

The road hugs *Pescadero Creek*, which is stocked weekly with rainbow trout, some of trophy size. The Army Engineers were pushing for a high dam across the creek that would have flooded out some wooded areas and parkland. There was much vocal opposition—the effect on fishing was one reason—and plans were at least temporarily halted.

From Pebble Beach To Año Nuevo State Reserve and the Santa Cruz County Line

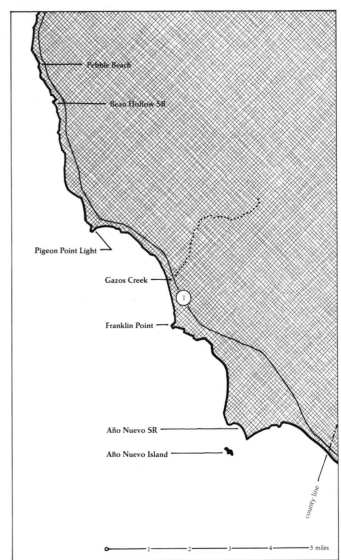

Pebble Beach

Bean Hollow SB

Pigeon Point Light

Gazos Creek

Franklin Point

Año Nuevo SR

Año Nuevo Island

county line

1————2————3————4————5 miles

P*EBBLE BEACH*, 1.5 miles south of Pescadero Beach on Highway 1, is famous for agates, jasper, carnelians, and other small, sea-polished stones, and this tiny beach also has a rocky area that the sea has pummeled into beautiful free-form sculptures. But the pebbles draw most people. Back in 1867, a reporter wrote that wagonloads of guests were taken to Pebble Beach daily from the thriving Swanton House hotel in Pescadero. "At the beach," he continued, "they pass the day buried in pebbles. From the cliff above a full view of the scene may be had, which is ridiculous in the extreme. Imagine a dozen females, some in bloomers and some without, some with long, some with short dresses, high boots and low-cut gaiters, straw hats, green veils, bandannas and the inevitable Shaker—lying about in every conceivable position, some on their knees and hands, others flat on their stomachs, with hands busy, feet stretched out and heads half buried in holes they have made in the beach . . ."

The supply of pebbles had diminished somewhat and it is supposed to be illegal to take any now. One good thing: in concentrating on pebbles, people have refrained from stripping the nearby tidepools of their sea inhabitants.

Many dedicated rockhounds turn up their noses at beach pebbles, but these pebbles can be incredibly beautiful. Most are in the quartz family and are not pure minerals but aggregate rocks. One reason for the confusion of names is that people picked up pretty pebbles and gave them names before scientists came along with their classification systems.

You can often find translucent pebbles of pure quartz. Agates of various types—quartz banded with impurities of different colors—are also common. So is jasper, an opaque quartz that ranges from rich red or yellow to dark green. Chances are that the "jade" you find will actually be jasper—or else serpentine.

Rock hunting is best at low tide, and the best season is winter or early spring, when deposits of sand on the beaches are low.

You can find *fossils* on the beaches or, more often, in hunks of sandstone that have broken off the cliffs. One way to preserve them is to scrub away dirt with a soft brush and coat them thinly with lacquer.

As for polishing pebbles, tumbling can take weeks. A quicker way is to use an emery cloth and scouring powder, followed by a thin coat of colorless lacquer (or hair spray with a lacquer base). This treatment may add a faintly yellow glint but will save time.

If pebbles don't interest you, try surf casting, rock fishing, or abalone picking here.

Arroyo de los Frijoles (or Bean Hollow), one mile south, is actually two pleasant, small but sandy beaches with good tidepools nearby. Try rock fishing, surf casting or abalone picking. If you're bik-

Bean Hollow beaches

ing, the Bean Hollow Road to Pescadero is noncongested and pleasant.

Next on Highway 1 you'll see a cluster of abandoned military barracks on what is now private property. The big Muzzi ranch, inland, across the highway near Pigeon Point, sells freshly picked beans and artichokes in season.

Pigeon Point

Pigeon Point, with its photogenic lighthouse, is about 3.5 miles farther south. Besides being picturesque, Pigeon Point is a favorite of skin divers, and you can also surf cast, rock fish, and pick abalone here. At low tide the tidepools are worth a look.

The *lighthouse* was built in 1872 with bricks brought around the Horn. The powerful lens, made of 1008 pieces of glass, was used first in New England and later at Fort Sumter in South Carolina, where it was buried in sand to protect it during the Civil War. Visitors are no longer admitted to the tower to see the six-foot-thick brick base and the weight and cable that originally operated the lens. The rope was wound by hand, so if power failed it could still be used. However, since the lighthouse

youth hostel

and buildings are now a *youth hostel*, it is possible to enter the grounds (415/879-0633).

At one time Pigeon Point could nearly have been called a port town. It boasted a whaling station plus a dozen cottages for the Portuguese whalers. In a small cove on the lee side, ships could be warped and loaded by means of cables—and later by a wharf with a swinging chute.

In the shadow of the lighthouse, local

The lighthouse at Pigeon Point is now a youth hostel, a favorite rendezvous for skindivers and abalone fishermen.

oysters have made their comeback, prodded along by the *Pigeon Point Shellfish Hatchery.* The company breeds oysters, imports and grows algae for their food, and, when the tiny oysters are no larger than sesame seeds, ships them throughout the world. Many of the oysters grown to maturity in Humboldt Bay near Eureka are sent here to be placed in filtered sea water for several weeks to clean them out. They are then washed and shipped to local markets and restaurants. Eventually the hatchery hopes to help other firms raise oysters and other sea crops.

shipwrecks   As you look at the surf churning over the reefs here, it's easy to see how the clipper ship *Carrier Pigeon* hit the rocks and broke in two in June, 1853—a rather dramatic way of getting her name on the map. Another ship, the *Seabird*, was sent from San Francisco to conduct salvage operations. She, too, fell victim to the raging sea. Leaking badly, the second ship was grounded at Año Nuevo, farther south.

In fact, there have been dozens of wrecks up and down this stretch of coast— one estimate is a hundred—and each shipwreck left its particular flotsam. As recently as eight years ago enough lumber to build several houses washed onto San Mateo beaches. Other cargoes littering the shore have been firecrackers, ginger jars, lichi nuts, and tea. From a cargo of toys, dolls bobbed up in tidepools for years. Another rescued cargo of colorful thread was stretched over scores of bushes to dry.

Probably the biggest throng of spectators—a dubious honor—watched while the three-masted jinx ship *New York* grounded in the breakers at the foot of Kelly Avenue in Half Moon Bay, on March 13, 1898. A gale at sea had torn away much of her rigging and the ship lurked off the coast for several days before managing to ground herself. When word of the event got around, almost everyone in Half Moon Bay rushed down to look. Housewives left their mops, farmers left their plows, others left barstools and stores. Part of the cargo was opium, wine, tea, and silks, since the ship had come from the Orient. She also carried quantities of rice and tapioca, which soon swelled in the water and helped burst open the hatch covers. A postscript: in the Vallejo house in Half Moon Bay is a cabinet full of bright Chinese porcelain from this shipwreck, given to Fred Vallejo's aunt, then a young lady, for helping protect the salvage.

As for Pigeon Point wrecks, on November 21, 1868, the American sailing ship *Hellespont*, carrying a cargo of coal, crashed off the point. Portuguese whalers helped to rescue the seven who survived out of the crew of ninety.

On August 29, 1929, an oil tanker rammed the passenger steamer *San Juan* off Pigeon Point. Eighty-seven persons died; forty-two were saved. (Other shipwrecks are discussed on page 98.)

Gazos Creek Access   *Gazos Creek Access*, two miles south, has grass-covered dunes, a few nooks protected from the blast of the wind, and primitive latrines. Surf casting is about the only ocean fishing possible here.

Small streams wind down from the mountains to the Pacific all along the coastside, but good catches of fish are rare after the first of the trout season. An exception is *Gazos Creek*, which is stocked occasionally with rainbow trout. Starting on the Saturday nearest to May 1 and continuing through September, Fish and Game people bring in the planting trucks to accessible areas. They vary their schedule to foil fishermen who might try to follow the trucks.

Many *salmon* and *steelhead* used to enter several coastside streams to spawn—that is, those that escaped the seals and sea lions lying in wait outside the streams' mouths. With the increase of dams, pollution, and other dubious benefits of civilization, however, these fish rarely venture into streams and rivers on their own any more. When they do, visitors and natives sometimes help carry them in buckets upstream.

Recently, in an attempt to recapture some prepollution runs, yearling *silver salmon* were planted in Gazos Creek, in the hope that they would migrate to the ocean and return to the stream to spawn two years later. To establish self-perpetuating runs, the planting was done for three consecutive springs. A private firm, Silver King Oceanic Farms, has spent $100,000 to stock salmon and steelhead in Waddell Creek and let them grow in the ocean. At last report, the effort is proving successful.

Gazos Creek Beach House

Back on Highway 1, on the landward side, you'll see that the former Pinkey's, now the *Gazos Creek Beach House*, still peddles gas (valuable along this isolated area) but it's worth a stop even if your tank is full. The restaurant-bar is now an oasis where you can stoke up on generally excellent breakfasts, lunches, and (on weekends) dinners. More good news: the drinks

This old ranch house along Gazos Creek is now abandoned but still recalls the bucolic charms of yesterday.

pack a wallop and you'll actually find clams in the clam chowder.

Gazos Ranch

Deserted *Gazos Ranch*, next south, has buildings dating from 1862, and the room at the rear of the two-story main house was built in 1896 of lumber salvaged from the wreck of the *Columbia*. The Frank Latta's sold out to Campbell Soup interests, and the Indian museum and beach facilities they operated are no more. However, the beautiful beach and sand dunes are still in their natural state because plans to put in recreational facilities were prohibited by zoning regulations.

Cloverdale Road

If you're driving north and don't mind getting your car dusty, you might enjoy the old farmhouses and quiet scenes along the *Gazos Creek–Cloverdale Road*, which goes inland at Butano Park and ends near Pescadero. Staying on the Gazos Creek

Franklin Point

Road itself to its end, however, is only for the hardy.

Franklin Point, named after a famous shipwreck, is just south of Gazos Creek.

On January 17, 1865, the clipper ship *Sir John Franklin* of Baltimore was proceeding up the California coast by dead reckoning. After passing rocky Año Nuevo Point, the ship hit the rock ledge that juts out at Franklin Point, and broke in two. Twelve were lost in the heavy seas. Survivors claimed that so much cargo was strewn about that they could run along the tops of the boxes on their way to shore.

Years later, pioneer Pablo Vasquez recalled that the beach was covered with boxes, wagons, pianos, and some of the three hundred kegs of spirits the ship had carried. He insisted, however, that he and many others were most delighted with the cans of turkey, chicken, lobster, oysters, and other gourmet foods that washed ashore.

Most fishermen and beachcombers who visit Franklin Point now are unaware that the remains of the ship and part of her crew lie beneath the dunes. But shifting sands at the point of land nearest the shipwreck scene occasionally uncover a headstone. Who placed it there no one knows. It reads:

> To the Memory of Edward Church of Baltimore, Md. Age 16 years, and the ten other seamen lost on Ship Sir John Franklin January 17, 1865.

Whether or not you see this headstone or find a piece of a shipwreck, hiking is pleasant in this area, especially at low tide.

One of the oldest homes on the coastside was built in 1851 by Isaac Graham, a relative of Daniel Boone. It still stands on *White House Creek Road,* surrounded by eucalyptus trees.

Green Oaks Ranch, four miles south of Gazos Creek, was donated to San Mateo County by Mrs. Catherine Steele as a historical site and recreational area. But manpower and money are needed to restore the beautiful old ranch house, the barn built without nails, and the trophy room. It would take even more to maintain the buildings and the thirteen acres of gardens, orchards, and stream. Since this is a banana belt and the weather is sunny most of the year, plants, trees and flowers flourish—especially roses and rhododendrons. Still, collecting garbage is just part of it all. So the county (or state) is often in a quandary. Since manpower and money are limited, should all the effort go into opening up new sites or improving parks already in existence? It's a hard decision, and so far Green Oaks has lost out.

A state facility that has not lost out is *Año Nuevo State Reserve.*

> "And how far is it to Point Año Nuevo?" a traveler near Pescadero asked an old Indian.
>
> "Oh, señor, it must be a very long way! I think it is in the neighborhood of the other world." (Albert S. Evans, 1873, in *Ala California*)

In addition to its 360-degree views of crashing surf and coastside mountains,

**Año Nuevo
State
Reserve**

Año Nuevo State Reserve, just north of the Santa Cruz County line, is probably the most interesting natural area along the entire San Mateo coast. Yet before 1970 few people had sampled its windswept attractions. These include acres of wildflowers, deep sand dunes that may cover Indian shell mounds, and ocean beaches that vary from rocky to sandy to sea-debris covered. The main attraction, however, is the noisy collection of sea birds and sea mammals within camera range. The stars of this wild menagerie, the gigantic elephant seals— the world's most improbable animals— battle, mate, and have their pups right on Año Nuevo Point.

If you miss the main elephant seal action, which takes place from December 1 through March, there's still plenty to see and do to make the admission fee of a $2.00 per car worthwhile. If the wind isn't whipping sand and fog into your face, you can sunbathe and picnic on the first long beach, which is sprinkled with rocks and fossils. (Don't pick up any fossils or anything else from the state beaches; it's illegal. Leave them for others to enjoy, too.) Surfers usually find the waves here to their liking, especially in the summer when other beaches may be disappointing. And if you're interested in geology, you'll pass over five earthquake faults if you walk from the hill at New Year's Creek to the end of the point. You can spot the faults by the wide streaks of ground-up rocks they produced; it's easier to see the faults from the beach.

Almost every variety of fishing is excellent off Año Nuevo rocks and beaches.

The seals and sea lions are aware of this, as are the party boats and skiffs from Santa Cruz that fish offshore. The rocky shelf areas are productive for abalone, poke poling for eels, and rock fishing. This is also one of the few coastside spots where you can scratch for littleneck clams at a minus tide, although state park officials are frowning on clamming here now.

wildlife As for animals, you're sure to see cotton-tailed rabbits hopping about and you may disturb some mule deer or even a coyote. Look closely at the tracks of birds and animals—besides those of *homo sapiens*—in the dusty paths and sand dunes.

plant life In spring the yellow and purple lupine, orange-gold poppies, and other wildflowers put on a spectacular show, but even in a parched late summer, the flowers and plants are interesting. Since the area is usually extremely windy, you can admire the methods the plants use to adapt. The coyote bush, for instance, has small tough leaves, as do the lupines. Where the wind is even fiercer, the plants hug the ground. Many plants, like the "live forevers," have fuzzy leaves to catch moisture in the fog. Where the sun can be intense among the sand dunes, the leaves may be almost silvery to reflect away the heat, and the leaves of verbena attract sand to help the plant retain its moisture. Almost all plants in the arid areas have taproots at least ten feet long, and many produce seed pods that explode. The sea rockets, plants with small lavender flowers, go even further, producing two-stage rockets containing seeds that can survive in salt water for up to eleven days.

A surfer catches a wave just south of Año Nuevo Point, a popular spot with the surfboard set.

Gradually, with the help of the willows that are growing near the manmade pond, enough plants are taking root to indicate that the sand dunes will eventually be stabilized. Other plants include the Indian paintbrush, with its red flower from which "love tea" can be made. The showy Hooker's primrose has big yellow flowers, and the "pearly everlasting" has dense white flower heads (its dried leaves are used for medicinal purposes). English plaintain—which springs up in walked-on-areas—has longitudinal ribs and small flowers. Its seeds, as well as the spicy wild radish, can be eaten.

As for birds, Año Nuevo is a bird-watcher's paradise. Soon after you start along the path from the parking area, you'll see cormorants, pelicans, and pigeon guillimots sitting on the weirdly shaped rocks in the ocean (one rock looks like a submarine). You can identify the guillimots by their bright-red feet and clownish behavior. In the spring and summer you'll glimpse cormorants nesting on the sides of bluffs so steep it's hard to see how they and the babies don't fall off. Besides these birds and the usual gulls, plovers sit in the sand, swallows dart after

bird life

insects, sparrows sing, and a pair of live-in marsh hawks circle above looking for field mice. (You'll see many mice burrows along the way.) Coots bring up their families in the pond, which was put in by the Steeles when this was working farmland but is now a crucial part of the area's ecology and an attraction to many birds. Even in the prepond era, however, Año Nuevo was on the flyway; rangers report that almost every sea bird that migrates has been spotted, and many land birds as well—a total of more than 230 species! Even if you're not a birdwatcher you have to be impressed with a number of varieties that have winged over this area. Some of the rarest include the golden eagle, the magnificent frigate bird, the American redstart, the red phalarope, and the whistling swan.

birds that breed at Año Nuevo

Birds that breed on Año Nuevo Island include black oyster-catchers, Brandt's cormorants, western gulls, and house finches.

Many species of birds breed on the mainland: belted kingfishers, black swifts, pelagic cormorants, pintails, common teals, ruddy ducks, marsh hawks, American kestrels, California quail, pigeon guillemot, American coots, snowy plovers, kildeer, marbled murrelets, rock doves, barn or great horned owls, black phoebes, many varieties of swallows, chickadees, bushtits, wrentits, house wrens, mockingbirds and California thrashers, hermit thrushes, loggerhead shrikes, house sparrows, red-winged and Brewer's blackbirds, American goldfinch, rufous-sides or brown towhees, dark-eyed juncos, and

Cormorants nest on the precipitous cliffs at Año Nuevo Point, a good place to watch these feathered divers.

many sparrows including Savannah, white crowned and song sparrows.

When you reach the tip of Año Nuevo Point, after floundering through or by the sand dunes, adjust your binoculars so you can enjoy the antics of the seals and sea lions on Año Nuevo Island. However—a warning! Many people have lost their lives trying to make it out through the treacherous surf at minus tide. If the day is at all clear you'll see and certainly hear plenty from shore, even when many of the elephant seals are off somewhere else.

the pinniped crowd

In the Indian era, wolves, mountain lions, and grizzly bears hunted down most visiting seals and sea lions. These predators, along with the Indians, are gone now, although there have been reports of mountain lions back in the coastal hills. So today's visitors can see anywhere from a few hundred to thousands of pinnipeds clustered on Año Nuevo Island or swimming in the turbulent waters offshore. Perhaps you'll see adolescent elephant seal bulls testing their prowess for battle. Or you may see California sea lions, often erroneously called seals, happily body surfing. (Remember, unlike the sea lion, a seal has no ears, and because its flipper is fixed behind like a tail, it has to flop or undulate forward like a worm.) You may glimpse a few smaller (up to five hundred pounds) harbor seals out on the rocky shoals. They're also known as leopard seals because of their spots. Even rarer here are fur seals and hair seals which have hairy front flippers.

To help you identify these and the many other animals and plants in Año Nuevo State Reserve, a ranger often leads nature walks during summer weekends at 10 A.M. and 1 P.M. Call 415/879-0227 to verify.

You're almost sure to see and hear the tawny-colored Steller sea lions on the island. They're bigger and noisier than California sea lions and have smooth, sloping brows plus, of course, those external ears. Steller sea lion bulls can weigh a ton.

It's the elephant seal crowd, however, that steals the show at Año Nuevo beaches, especially since they now carry on right on the point. The bulls arrive in early December to stake out their territory. The females join them in late December, Pups from last year's matings are born in January. When the babies are weaned in February, the new matings commence with much sound and fury.

elephant seals

A full-grown elephant seal bull can weigh from two to four tons. He's quite unattractive, a dirty gray color with a thick cracked neck and a snout, or proboscis, that helps him let out a bellow that can be heard for miles. That sound is hard to describe—it's something between an elephant's roar and the sound of a hollow log being struck in a deep tunnel. The fawn-colored females are docile (or lazy?), and much smaller, with large liquid, long-suffering eyes. When dozing away, side by side, the females can look like oversized cigars, and the babies are called weenies.

The bulls put up prodigious battles to keep other bulls out of their territories so they can mate with these listless females. When challenged, the bulls heave their massive cracked heads, trumpet that uncanny sound, and start to pummel each other with their heads and snouts. The loser shrivels up his nose and retreats. The ultimate winner of a series of battles may end up with a harem of fifty or more cows and is known as the alpha bull. All the time these activities are going on, the elephant seals don't eat. The bulls are afraid to leave their territories and the females are afraid their pups may be lost or squashed accidentally by a big bull.

When you see hundreds of elephant seals crowding the island and dozing on point beaches, it's hard to realize that before the turn of the century these ponderous mammals were hunted for their blubber to the edge of extinction. A few survived on a lonely island off Baja California, and these finally spread up the coast from isolated Southern California rookeries to Año Nuevo.

Now Año Nuevo is the only place in the world where elephant seals can be safely seen close up by hundreds of visitors. How this came about is a saga of trial, error, and eventual success.

Because so many ships were wrecked off the island's rocky shoals, the government bought Año Nuevo Island in 1870 and erected a lighthouse. The lighthouse was abandoned in 1948 and seals and sea lions moved in—some even into the building. One official still remembers the aroma of the six-hundred-pound sea lion who had expired in a bathtub.

In 1958 the State of California purchased Año Nuevo Island and enough of the mainland to provide access. There was even some talk about the state selling out until the importance of this isolated area as a natural habitat for pinnipeds was realized. So, in 1967 the state officially declared the island a scientific and scenic reserve. To help protect the animals, the University of California at Santa Cruz was designated as a responsible lessee. When

Año Nuevo Lighthouse

A bull elephant seal at Año Nuevo State Preserve takes a belly-up siesta while waiting for his harem.

the waters were calm enough, a few professors and students of marine biology at the University would put out to the island in a rubber boat to study the animals from blinds. To make spotting easier, the huge animals were daubed with identifying marks—a mixture of Lady Clairol Blue hair dye with 30 percent peroxide applied with a stick. As the elephant seal population exploded on the island, a few bachelors swam ashore to the mainland, then called "Loser's Beach." By 1973, thirty-eight elephant seals, including several battling bulls, have moved to the beach.

In December of that year, *Sunset Magazine* recommended this spectacle to readers. Suddenly hundreds, and then thousands of people trampled their way through the fragile dunes to the point beaches, milled about the seals within bit-

elephant seal spectacle

ing distance, and threw rocks at sleeping bulls to get action photographs.

The state had to do something to protect both the seals and the people, but what? The reserve couldn't be placed off limits; there just weren't sufficient funds or personnel to close it and police it. Only one ranger, who sometimes felt he was nothing but a glorified garbage collector, stopped here part time. Finally, Roger Werts, who took over as head of the Northern San Mateo Coast State Parks, worked out a way for students from nearby West Valley College in Saratoga to take part in a ranger trainee program. So when the avalanche of visitors began, he stationed two rangers and a few students in the parking lot to control visitor access.

Werts, a tall, craggy man and somewhat of a hero to his rangers, started his career at Humboldt State College, majoring in wildlife management. Before he graduated a friend talked him into taking the examination for entry into the state park system. Twenty years later he still likes to deal with people and help protect preserves and parks so that visitors can "keep from going stir crazy" in crowded cities. Even if they don't go to the parks, Werts believes just knowing that there is open public land out there is important.

As more and more people came, traffic snarls developed and tempers flared. Something else had to be done. Werts turned to the university at Santa Cruz to ask whether students might be interested in assisting the park ranger staff in explaining and protecting the seals, flora, and other fauna. After intensive training, a few stu-

dent guides were put to work in early 1976. Now, twenty-seven guided natural history walks are conducted daily throughout the elephant seal season by student tour guides trained in elephant seal biology, the natural history of local flora, fauna, and geology; local cultural history; and interpretive skills.

natural-history tours

Reserve early to get in on these tours; they're usually filled before November ends. From October 1, phone Año Nuevo State Reserve (415/879-0227 or 415/879-0228). If space is available on the date you want you'll receive confirmation by mail.

how to reserve

Even if these reservations are filled, all

A young cow elephant seal poses daintily for her portrait.

is not lost. SamTrans runs at least two "Elephant Seal Special" buses a day from Mid-December to early March. Prepaid reservations for the five-hour roundtrip ride from San Mateo and a guarantee you'll be admitted to the state tours are accepted on a first-come-first-served basis at SamTrans, 400 S. El Camino, San Mateo, CA 94402. Alternatively, on weekdays you can call 415/348-SEAL, the SamTrans tour reservation number. Roundtrip fare is $5.00. The Elephant Seal Special leaves from the Hillsdale Shopping Center and picks up additional passengers at 10 A.M. in Half Moon Bay at the SamTrans bus stop shelter on Highway 92 just off Highway 1. Also the Santa Cruz Metropolitan Transit district runs Elephant Seal Tours. Their address is 230 Walnut Street, Santa Cruz, CA 95060 (408/425-8600).

history   Año Nuevo State Reserve also had a lot of history going for it. Vizcaino, who sailed by on New Year's Day, 1603, named it Punta del Año Nuevo.

Ever since, because of its hidden reefs, heavy fogs and turbulent waters, the point has claimed many lives, some involving lighthouse personnel. The steamer *Los Angeles*, passing in April 1883, noticed that the lighthouse fog signal was not operating and that the ensign was flying upside down as a signal of distress. When they investigated they found that the station

shipwrecks   crew had been drowned off a dory; only wives and children were left.

In November 1886, the British bark *Coya*, with a cargo of coal, hit a hidden reef at Año Nuevo, turned broadside, and

sank. Three were saved of the twenty passengers and a crew of ten.

On April 10, 1887 the *H. W. Seaver*, a 27-year-old sailing ship, whose rotten hull had been painted over, went aground. Three crewmen died in the heavy surf at Año Nuevo Beach. Sequel: seventy-eight years later, a man strolling on the beach after a storm discovered a rusted bowsprit band. Searching through records at the San Francisco Maritime Museum, he found that the *H. W. Seaver* had disappeared mysteriously from official records in about 1887. Further searching turned up an account of the wreck in a Santa Cruz weekly newspaper.

On December 20, 1887, the *San Vicente* was wrecked. Its cargo of empty lime barrels caught fire at sea outside Point Año Nuevo, and eighteen died.

On July 14, 1896, due to the captain's carelessness, the *Columbia* almost struck the lighthouse at Año Nuevo. Part of the ship's cargo was white paint, starting the rumor that much of this cargo found its way to Pescadero, which is why Pescadero houses are usually painted white. Sequel: the rear of one of the old buildings at the old Gazos Ranch (now belonging to the Campbell Soup interest) was built of lumber salvaged from this wreck.

The old light station is abandoned now. While it was still occupied, the keeper complained that young sea lion pups were overrunning his house. On one occasion a killer whale stirred up the mammals so much they forced their way into every room.

According to Frank Stanger's fascinating book *South From San Francisco*, when the foghorn of the first light station first blasted in May, 1872, all the cows on the neighboring Steele ranch stampeded down to the beach. Mrs. Steele commented that the cows must have thought there was a very wonderful bull down there.

Steele family lore   Many well-kept-up farms from the Steele Brothers' dairy empire still remain in the Año Nuevo area. Against advice, the Steele clan first dairied at cold, windswept Point Reyes. This was so successful they bought similar land, part of the original Rancho Punto Año Nuevo, from Loren Coburn. Isaac Steele started his home at Green Oaks in 1862, and cousin, R. E. (Renneslear) Steele, built in Cascade Creek that year. By 1869 most of the eleven dairies nearby were operated or leased by the Steeles. One brother became a general in the Union Army, but the Steeles were most famous for the cheese, nearly four thousand pounds and twenty feet in circumference, that was auctioned off in San Francisco for the benefit of the Union Army.

Indian lore   Long before the Steeles settled and before the Spanish explorers and missionaries arrived in the 1700s, thousands of Indians lived near or visited Año Nuevo Point and Island. You'll see evidence of their activities near the point when you reach the sand dunes, for they cover Indian shell mounds. Shell mounds are the dumps where Indians threw away mussel, clam, oyster, and abalone shells from their daily fare. Archaeologists who excavate such mounds, which they call kitchen middens,

can date the layers by the implements and ornaments they find. You can see fragments of the shells today, and when the wind whips enough sand off the mounds it may uncover fragments of stone arrowheads or stone tools.

Note: Digging in shell mounds on Año Nuevo Point or in any other area in or outside a state park is illegal. So it follows that the law prohibits removal of any items such as broken shells, arrow chips, or other Indian artifacts. If you do stumble across a shell mound anywhere, notify a responsible institution, a nearby college or university. If your discovery lies along the San Mateo coastline, notify the San Mateo Historical Association (415/341-6161, extension 394).

The abundance of live mollusks that resulted in all those shell mounds supported one of the largest populations of Indians that existed in California before the arrival of the whiteskins. When Portola's party stumbled up the coast and inadvertently discovered San Francisco Bay, they saw Indian villages near almost every creek mouth. But these coast Indians were among the first to be felled by broken spirits and imported diseases.

Almost nothing except the shell mounds remains of the thousands of Indians who lived on the coastside for ten to fifteen thousand years or more. A few intricately crafted baskets and artifacts sit in museums. The County Historical Museum at the College of San Mateo, 1700 West Hillsdale Boulevard, San Mateo, has a few. So does the Santa Cruz City Museum, at 1305 East Cliff Drive in Santa Cruz.

Only a handful of Costanoan (coast) Indians survive. Many lived with and as Mexicans so long they forgot old customs, and these customs are worth mentioning.

The Indians didn't have to garden, since seafood, some wild game, acorns, certain seeds, berries, and insects were plentiful. A house was a hole in the ground covered with a dome-shaped frame and thatched with tule or grass. The men took sweat baths in a temescal, or subterranean oven, the central feature of many villages. Early travelers report that the women scratched themselves frequently. They weren't allowed in the temescal.

Dressing was easy. Males usually didn't. Seen from a distance, the men often appeared to be wearing costumes with wide horizontal stripes. Close up, it became obvious the stripes were merely painted on naked skin. In cold weather one might carry a firebrand for warmth, don an animal-skin cape, or just daub on mud. For ceremonies they added feathered headdresses. Women wore aprons, front and back, plus capes over their shoulders, and some decorated their faces with tattoos.

Cooking was complicated. Before even starting to make *pinole* (a meal made from parched seeds of various native plants), they would throw a handful of the seeds to the sun, moon, or sky, saying, "I send you this so that another year you will give me greater abundance." Acorn meal was put in watertight baskets and heated stones were thrown in to cook the meal.

Tools were of bone, shells, or stone that had been tediously shaped by grinding with sand and hard rock. Arrowheads and spearheads were chipped from quartz, which was plentiful. Light rafts were made of tules or reeds tied in bundles, and these craft were strong enough to be paddled out to sea.

Not too many decades ago these Indians were considered backward or inferior. Now quite a few anthropologists, philosophers, and others admire the Indian way of life. The fact that so little material remains from their era is perhaps a tribute. They left the land as their ancestors had found it, unscarred, unsacked, and undepleted.

From the San Mateo County Line to the Outskirts of Santa Cruz

7

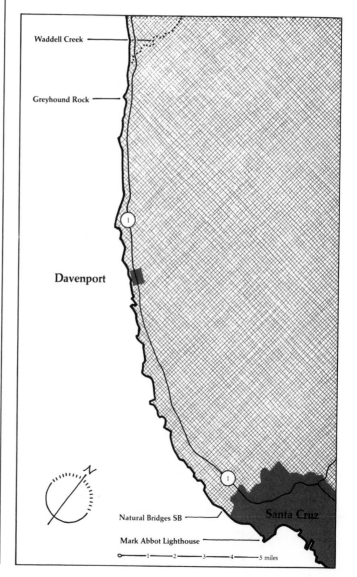

Waddell Creek

Greyhound Rock

Davenport

Natural Bridges SB

Mark Abbot Lighthouse

Santa Cruz

0 — 1 — 2 — 3 — 4 — 5 miles

W*ADDELL CREEK*, with its attractive beach, is just south of the Santa Cruz County line and the chalk mountains. Before Highway 1 was scraped out of these steep, crumbling bluffs, stage coaches had to wait for low tide before they could race across the sand. Because slides cut off the route so often, Pescadero seceded from Santa Cruz County and joined San Mateo County. Waddell, an early pioneer, erected a wharf at Año Nuevo as a shipping point for lumber from his mill, but his career was cut short. He met an early death after encountering a grizzly bear.

On the south side of Waddell Creek is an impressive farm owned by the Hoover family. The north side of the creek is now part of the Big Basin Redwoods State Park, and—at last!—you can hike from park headquarters on a rough but scenic drop to the ocean. The Sempervirens Fund, which was largely responsible for this beautiful trail, has produced two maps that describe the trail's many attractions. Write to Sempervirens, P.O. Box 1141, Los Altos, CA 94022 for Skyline-to-the-Sea Trail Maps 1 and 2, enclosing 70¢ and a self-addressed envelope.

trail from Big Basin to ocean

The trail often skirts the creek and its many waterfalls. (Yes, you can sit in some waterfalls, and the sensation is great). There are three backpack trail camps in the lower Waddell area; the overnight charge is 50¢ per person per night. Reserve camping space through Big Basin State Park, (408/338-6132). If you end your hike on Highway 1 at Waddell Creek you can take the Route 41–Davenport bus back to Santa Cruz.

On the Waddell beach area you can enjoy beachcombing and surf casting, and campers have been known to stay overnight here.

You can see some inland scenery on the way to the *Big Creek Pottery*, a gallery and live-in pottery school. Turn sharply left on Swanton Road just past the Big Creek Lumber Company. If you reach Greyhound Rock you've gone too far, but don't worry. Since the turnoff is so sharp, many drivers prefer to turn around at Greyhound Rock. Drive up about a mile on the corkscrew Swanton Road until you spot the cluster of beautifully remodeled old redwood buildings and the yellow Rennaissance flag.

Swanton Road

The Pottery is run by Bruce McDougal, who lives here year-round with his family. The gallery is open by appointment (408/423-4402). The school operates only during the summer. When not teaching or helping run the new restaurant-pottery gallery in Davenport, Bruce and his wife, Marcia, work on their own pottery. One of the buildings, dating from the 1860s, was once used to produce cheese. The whole set-up, with its huge trees and sloping fields, is worth the drive.

potteries

Scott Creek Pottery, smaller than Big Creek, is farther inland on Swanton Road, and according to rumor, more potters contemplate moving into the general area.

Scott Creek

The Santa Cruz Chamber of Commerce insists you can catch trout, crappie, bluegill, black bass, and catfish at *Scott Creek*. Even if you don't visit the potteries, watch for the several abrupt changes of vegetation on Swanton Road, from low-lying shoreline shrubs to great redwoods. Many wild animals still roam these mountains, and water ouzels (dippers), chunky little birds that walk under water, nest behind waterfalls on some of the streams. However, much of this country is on private property, strictly fenced off. Swanton Road continues through more forested semi-isolated territory until it eventually rejoins Highway 1 farther south.

Hang glider enthusiasts sometimes use the windy bluffs near here to launch their gossamer craft out over the ocean.

Greyhound Rock

Greyhound Rock, a state fish and game reserve, is the next access to the ocean on Highway 1. On weekends the parking lot is usually jammed with the cars of rock fishermen, and some stay overnight. The area has primitive latrines and a scattering of overflowing garbage cans. Besides rock fishing, surf netting and skindiving are popular here. Dress warmly if you plan to fish; that wind off the ocean can cut like a fish knife.

Davenport

For sixty-five years *Davenport* (population 300) could be spotted a mile away by the pall of cement dust that belched from the factory smokestack and covered fields, cars, and roofs. Antipollution officials got tough, and in 1971 the factory spent a lot of money for a cure. Now housewives who hang out their wash can expect it to stay moderately clean, and some people insist that even the weather has improved. The Davenport cement plant utilizes a limestone quarry nearby.

Davenport and Davenport Landing were famous decades ago for whaling. The whalers are gone, but the whales return each year, usually from the last of November into February. The high bluffs overlooking the ocean here are excellent vantage points for watching the migration of these huge mammals. Many Portuguese who live in Davenport are descendants of early whalers. Theirs was an exciting occupation. When a whale was spotted, small double-ended boats, like those still used in the Azores, were launched through the surf and directed by spotters on the cliff top, who ran signal flags up a flagpole. After the whale was harpooned, it was dragged ashore and the oil extracted right there.

early whaling

Businesses in Davenport strung along Highway 1 include a gas station, a saloon, and the new edition of Gregory's Country Store, which sells fishing gear, food, beer, and other necessities. It also calls itself a delicatessen from 10 to 4, but prices are high.

The new *Davenport Cash Store,* actually a restaurant-pottery shop and a gallery, occupies the corner where the original Davenport Cash Store once served as the hub of social and business life. The original burned down in the early 1950s. The current store, started by the McDougals of Big Creek Pottery, sells gift items and pottery, some made on the premises. The restaurant is popular; it's the only one for miles. It serves sand-

Davenport Cash Store

wiches, soups, salads, and daily specials, including a musician softly singing and playing a guitar. The "store" is open from 7 to 5 daily (408/423-4402).

local artisans Besides a beehive of potters, Davenport is home base for a growing number of artisans. David Boye, a knife maker (who will etch your knife handle on request) is at 17 San Vicente (408/426-6046). He is also author of a book on handmade knives. The Davenportmill, 433 Marine View Avenue, (408/423-8577), does large custom-woodwork including doors and table tops. The shop's sizeable collection of antique woodworking tools is worth a look. Across the street at 121 Marine View is the Jim Lundberg Studio (408/423-2532), which produces such blown-glass items as lampshades, paperweights, and goblets. Many of the studio's wares go on sale the three weekends before Christmas. Bud Bogle makes custom handmade furniture on First Avenue (408/426-1741), and there's even a t-shirt factory in town.

Aeolus Boat Works The *Aeolus Boat Works*, tucked into a dusty cul-de-sac inland and about two blocks down on the Old Coast Road is run by Bill Grunwald, an ex-fisherman, and is named after the Greek god of winds. The small boatworks specializes in mahogany dories. You can buy anything from a do-it-yourself kit for a few hundred dollars to a gentleman's rowing yacht of the Victorian period (for the person who can afford to go first class). This enterprise, in a building erected at the turn of the century, welcomes visitors Monday through Saturday. You can also find out about the dangerous

and exciting recreational rowing regattas here. The boatworks is open days (408/423-5681).

Downtown Davenport is so compact that when you're back off the highway you can't help but notice the rustic *St. Vincent de Paul's Church*, built of local cement in 1915. **St. Vincent de Paul's Church**

Just south of Davenport, a bluff above a small beach across the railroad tracks has a photogenic view. Some historians think the gully here is the one where explorer Portola's expedition lost a mule and many pots and pans on its march north. The drop to the beach is steep enough to make you believe that a mule might have trouble. Fishing from the south end of this beach is recommended at low tide only.

The Bonny Doon Road, one mile south of Davenport, wanders up to Felton and connects with State Route 9. Most tourist attractions around Felton are included in the Santa Cruz Fun Guide and other literature distributed by the Santa Cruz Chamber of Commerce. There are also a few resorts and restaurants off the beaten track. The *Trout Farm Inn*, 1500 Zayante Road, a short distance off the Graham Hill Road, has a pool, bar, and, as its name implies, trout-filled ponds for fishing. **Bonny Doon Road**

Among Felton's well-publicized attractions is the old *covered bridge* near the Zayante and Mount Hermon roads, a short distance east of Highway 9. Drive down a dirt road by a big fruit stand, park, and walk out onto the bridge. All you'll see **covered bridge at Felton**

The old covered bridge at Felton has been standing there since 1892, but no longer conveys traffic across the river.

are the shallows of the San Lorenzo River, but how many covered bridges have you walked through lately?

From Felton you can go north to Big Basin Redwoods State Park and through the tree-shadowed resort areas of Ben Lomond, Brookdale, and Boulder Creek. Or you can drive a short distance south to *Henry Cowell Redwoods State Park.* This 4000-acre park has a restaurant and gift shop, fifteen miles of trails, many picnic sites, and a 130-unit campground. Fees here are the same as for other developed state park campsites—$2.00 a car for day

Henry Cowell Redwoods State Park

use, $5.00 for overnights, $6.00 for trailers thirty-six feet or less; and 50 percent off these fees for seniors sixty-two or over. Hikers and bikers pay only 50¢ for overnight stays here.

Three hiking and riding trails take you into the semiwilderness area south and west of the campground. One easy jaunt leads you to the water tank for a panoramic view of the park and Santa Cruz. The Rincon Trail, which intersects with the Ridge Trail, starts from a parking lot alongside State Highway 9 at the park's south end. It passes by the Cathedral Redwoods, a ring of trees growing from a single base.

Redwood Grove, the most visited site in the park, has a self-guided nature path. Near the grove the picnic grounds overlook the *San Lorenzo River,* which is popular with swimmers or with fishermen during the fishing season, from mid-November to the end of February. When the winter runs begin, the banks are crowded with fishermen going after steelhead and silver salmon, which congregate at the river's mouth in Santa Cruz until winter rains raise the water level so they can migrate upstream to spawn.

Next door to the park, trains of the *Roaring Camp and Big Trees Narrow-Gauge Railroad* frequently toot by, belching purple smoke. Here you can visit a replica of a roaring camp town, then board the small train for a beautiful five-mile roundtrip through acres of redwoods.

Going south from the park, Route 9 follows the San Lorenzo River to industrial

commercial campgrounds

Santa Cruz. The twisting road was built for narrow cars of another era, but the scenery is worth the effort. As for *commercial campgrounds,* the River Grove Park, one mile south of Felton, has sixty campsites, hookups for trailers, and swimming. Smithwood's Resort, further south, has eighty-four campsites, trailer hookups, and swimming.

From Felton you can also take a side excursion to trout-filled Loch Lomond Reservoir. The area is thick with summer cottages and retirement hideaways, restaurants, souvenir shops selling redwood artifacts, resorts, and eateries. Sunnyview Lodge, a private park six miles wet of Boulder Creek on Basin Way, has twenty campsites and swimming.

Big Basin Redwood State Park

If you've driven this far (and the drive is almost as difficult if you start south from San Francisco on Skyline Boulevard) you should continue on to *Big Basin Redwoods State Park,* probably the best known and certainly the oldest California state park. It's well worth the extra twists and turns, since the park is tucked among impressive redwoods and deer come up to eat out of your hands (although the rangers are discouraging this). You'll see many waterfalls and varying natural environments, and that's just a start.

hiking trails

Hikers can enjoy more than thirty-five miles of hiking trails within the park. These include part of a fifteen-mile riding trail that will eventually form a loop. Many hiking trails follow streambeds through deep redwood forests; others climb ridges to vista points where you can see much of this unusual basin country and (perhaps) the ocean beyond. There's also a hiking trail that connects Big Basin Park with *Castle Rock State Park,* fourteen miles to the northeast, and the trail from Big Basin to the ocean.

A hundred and fifty-eight scenic picnic sites with tables and stoves scattered throughout this huge park are available on a first-come-first-served basis for $2.00 per car per day. Fees for 260 individual-family overnight sites are $5.00 per car, with a fifteen-day limit. Fees are 50 percent off for seniors sixty-two or over, and hikers or bikers can camp overnight for 50¢ each. It's safer to reserve ahead from your nearest Ticketron outlet or on a form from the Department of Parks and Recreation, P.O. Box 2390, Sacramento, CA 95811. It's worth the extra reservation charge to be sure your family will have a place to camp after that long tortuous drive.

If you haven't made the inland detour and are still heading south on Highway 1, you'll pass three small creeks that meander down to the ocean south of the Bonny Doon Road: Laguna Creek, Majors Creek, and Baldwin Creek. According to Santa Cruz publicity, all three may contain trout, crappies, bluegill, black bass, and catfish. Most fishing along this section of coast, however, is rock fishing, but getting to the ocean is a problem and the beaches are hazardous as well. You'll see miles of Brussels sprouts on bluffs above the ocean, but almost all roads leading west are posted with no-trespassing signs.

Beaver Nudist Beach

Beaver Beach, for oldtime nudists, is exactly three miles south of Davenport. "Look for the red, white, and blue mailbox." When too many curiosity seekers find this beach, the mailbox is mysteriously painted over and no one knows anything about a nudist beach. There are wider, more scenic beaches along the coastside, but if you want to tan every square inch, this is the place for you. If you do make it in, you must be twenty-one years old (or married or with parents). Women are admitted free; there's a modest fee for couples, and single men are charged the most.

To your right further along, near a granite company, is an adobe built in 1781 on the former Wilder Ranch near Wilder Creek. Candida Castro, a daughter of Joaquin Castro, and her Russian husband, Jose Bolcoff, who left a Siberian whaling ship in Monterey, lived long, happy lives here with their large family. The ranch and **Wilder Ranch State Park** adobe are now part of the new *Wilder Ranch State Park*. The park, however, will not be in operation for several years when the state budget will be stretched enough to pay for trail camps, walk-in and drive-in camps, picnic sites, and historic facilities. A planned Santa Cruz Youth Hostel in the park was cancelled.

Natural Bridges State Park The sign directing you to *Natural Bridges State Park* is next. The road turns in near the Wrigley Gum factory, past many large homes and tasteful industries. Eroded rock arches gave this park its name; unfortunately, the biggest arch collapsed in January 1980, and a wake was held. Pelicans, cormorants, gulls, and other sea birds still congregate on the remaining pillars, and the waves still thunder in to continue the erosion.

Natural Bridges Beach State Park still has an eroded sea arch, but the big natural bridge collapsed during the winter of 1980.

The park, open for day use only, is a small sanctuary of nature, from its ocean beach to its ¾-mile nature trail, which leads back into an area where you can imagine yourself to be hundreds of miles from civilization. You even pass a secret lagoon on this trail, where mallard ducks may be cutting a smooth, dark swath through the green water.

Monarch butterflies

The main attraction from mid-October through mid-March is a grove of eucalyptus trees that attract the beautiful orange and black Monarch butterflies. They may travel up to three thousand miles at speeds as great as thirty miles an hour to hang in dense golden clusters from the branches here. For only a short time, on calm, warm days, they may leave their protective clusters in order to feed on the eucalyptus blooms. Since a Monarch's life cycle is only nine months long, the ones that leave here for the trip north will never return. But in some mysterious way the instinct—or whatever—to return to these same trees is passed on to following generations. To honor the return of these colorful animals with the velvet wings the park usually holds a Welcome Back Monarch's Day on the second or third Saturday in October. Call 408/423-4609 to verify.

Center for Coastal Marine Studies

In the same general area and well worth a visit is the *University of California Center for Coastal Marine Studies*, also known as Long's Marine Laboratory (408/429-2464). From Highway 1 turn west on Western, right at the Wrigley Gum factory to Natural Bridges Drive, then right on Delaware by a picturesque lagoon to the entrance, just past a mobile home resort.

The center, on a cliff overlooking Monterey Bay, is open Wednesday and Friday from 10 A.M. to 12 noon, and Saturday and Sunday from 1 P.M. to 4 P.M. for free tours led by student docents. You'll see a small aquarium of local marine life and tanks where sharks and other sea animals are studied. There's even a "touch tank" where blind visitors and children can actually feel some of the smaller marine creatures. One of the highlights of the center is the skeleton of the largest creature ever to live on earth, the blue whale. The skeleton exhibit is of an 85-foot long fifty-year-old female that washed ashore several years ago near Pescadero.

University of California at Santa Cruz

The *University of California at Santa Cruz* is at the northwest corner of the city of Santa Cruz on two thousand acres of meadow and redwood forest overlooking the city and Monterey Bay. Turn inland at Bay Street and drive up. The weathered buildings near the main entrance are nearly a century old, relics of when the property was part of the Henry Cowell Ranch. Now the barn is a campus theater and the other buildings are all in use.

The university, which is geared mainly to undergraduates, hoped to enroll twenty-five thousand by 1990. At present eight colleges are open, and enrollment is about six thousand. The student body includes some older students attending through a reentry program. The colleges—in clusters with open land between—are the basic units of the campus. Each college is a self-contained complex of classrooms, meeting rooms, a dining hall, and residences for both students and faculty. Certain facilities—such as the library—are used by all. Each college has its own style and lifestyle. The theme of Kresge College, for example, is man and his environment, and other colleges are becoming more problem oriented, with some actually trying to solve problems of nearby communities. The caliber of students is high, but all is not perfect, even here. Some students

The campus of the University of California at Santa Cruz is an architectural delight, reflecting its sylvan setting.

complain about the "ivory tower" feeling. If they're trying to solve community problems, some say, why not live in the community rather than staying isolated together on this beautiful campus?

But in the new Center for Coastal Marine Studies enthusiasm is high. Students and faculty both carry on their studies and help manage several coastal areas, including *Long Marine Laboratory*.

College Eight at UCSC operates a seventeen-acre farm and a five-acre garden. Both projects employ organic gardening techniques, free from chemical products. Most of the produce goes to help supply the campus's unique *Whole Earth Restaurant*. In all, there are nine coffee houses and restaurants on the campus, all open to the public.

Back on Highway 1, you continue to the south and you're in Santa Cruz.

Before you switch gears or turn back, visit the *Mark Abbott Memorial lighthouse* on West Cliff Drive (take Fair Street in). It's on the dividing line between the Pacific Ocean and Monterey Bay, with sweeping views of the coastline. You can also watch a herd of sea lions just off shore on Seal Rock.

As for the *boardwalk*, can a century of tourists—two million a year—be wrong? All across the country amusement parks and boardwalks have turned out their lights and locked their gates, but the mile-long Beach and Boardwalk at Santa Cruz still attracts throngs (weekends after the Labor Day week until Memorial Day and every day after that through the summer). Of course, this isn't everyone's idea of fun, the screaming ride on the Giant Dipper roller coaster or operating an "Atomic Bomber" in the huge Arcade or swinging high up on the ferris wheel or visiting the Cocoanut Grove dance casino where big old-time bands still play on occasion, or buying chocolate-covered bananas or fluorescent seashells. But the crowds still come: couples arm in arm, families and even a small contingent of people who once spurned this form of entertainment and now consider it "camp." They realize that the Giant Dipper is now an endangered species and the Merry-go-round is a classic with its 62 horses plus two Roman chariots hand-carved by a Danish wood carver and its Ruth Band organ with 342 pipes. Most visitors insist that the beach itself is the main magnet, so as long as Santa Cruz has that sunny mile-long stretch of sand washed by surf, visi-

Mark Abbott Memorial lighthouse

Santa Cruz boardwalk

Mark Abbott Memorial Lighthouse stands at the official demarcation between Monterey Bay and the Pacific Ocean.

tors will be flocking to the boardwalk. In fact, the boardwalk has just put in a double-decker miniature golf course and plans to add convention facilities. For yearly operating schedule or rate information, phone 408/423-5590.

The Santa Cruz Wharf that juts out near one end of the beach also attracts its share of visitors who fish off its sides or take a party boat out here or eat seafood—but that's another story.

For more information on these and other attractions—in fact, for free folders on everything to do and see that's legal around Santa Cruz—contact the Convention & Visitor's Bureau, Civic Auditorium, P.O. Box 921, Santa Cruz, CA 95060 (408/423-6927).

More Santa Cruz information

By now you will have explored many miles of the uncrowded land between the mountains and the sea south of San Francisco to the outskirts of more crowded Santa Cruz. You will have met a sampling of the people who have made this area their home—a variety that includes farmers, artists, rangers, pioneers, retirees, and business entrepreneurs. Perhaps you have seen hawks soar, heard the roar of elephant seal bulls, felt the salt sting of surf, watched the mirrored colors of a sunset fade away on a lonely beach or basked in the sun at the Santa Cruz beach.

Whatever your experiences—if you have paused to look and listen—those moments will have made all the difference.

Index

Look up *your* interests